MY WEEKLY KOREAN VOCABULARY
BOOK 1

written & designed by
Talk To Me In Korean

MY WEEKLY KOREAN VOCABULARY BOOK 1
매일매일 단어 공부 1

1판 1쇄 · 1st edition published	2014. 3. 3.
개정판 1쇄 · 1st revised edition published	2025. 3. 10.

지은이 · Written by	Talk To Me In Korean
책임편집 · Edited by	안효진 Hyojin An, 스테파니 베이츠 Stephanie Bates
디자인 · Designed by	선윤아 Yoona Sun
삽화 · Illustrations by	"The Drawing Project" participants
녹음 · Voice Recordings by	Talk To Me In Korean
펴낸곳 · Published by	롱테일북스 Longtail Books
펴낸이 · Publisher	이수영 Suyoung Lee
편집 · Copy-edited by	정소이 Soyi Jeong
주소 · Address	04033 서울특별시 마포구 양화로 113, 3층(서교동, 순흥빌딩)
	3rd Floor, 113 Yanghwa-ro, Mapo-gu, Seoul, KOREA
이메일 · E-mail	editor@ltinc.net
ISBN	978-1-942791-55-3
권장 가격 · Suggested Retail Price	USD 29

TTMIK - TALK TO ME IN KOREAN

MY WEEKLY KOREAN
VOCABULARY

with 1600+ everyday sample expressions

매일매일
단어 공부

BOOK 1

Contents

HOW TO USE
MY WEEKLY KOREAN VOCABULARY

Learning vocabulary words is an essential part of the journey to learning and becoming fluent in a new language. Memorizing words is one thing, but actually understanding the words and being able to naturally apply them is another. This book is designed to bridge memorization and application together to help you efficiently learn some of the most essential Korean vocabulary words, no matter if you are just beginning to learn Korean or if you are almost as fluent as a native speaker.

With a new keyword presented each day, along with 20 expressions where the keyword is used, this book provides you the tools to help you expand your Korean vocabulary in just 12 weeks. Each expression is longer than the previous and is broken down in the "Notes" section to help you pick up new and related vocabulary and grammatical structures. (Please note that romanizations are only provided for the keywords.) Audio files are available for download if you would like to listen to recordings of every keyword and expression in this book.

My Weekly Korean Vocabulary Book 1

As in any language, it is inevitable to repeat certain words. Although the daily keywords are never repeated, you will find that some of the words in the related expressions are used quite frequently. The same related vocabulary words can appear in the "Notes" section up to 12 times, one time for each week. For example, if 가다 (to go) appears in Week 1 Day 1, there will be a note, as it is the first time it appears that week. If at any other point during Week 1 the word 가다 appears in an expression, no note will be provided. However, if 가다 shows up again in Week 2, there will be a note provided the first time it appears.

If you find that learning a new word and 20 related expressions each day to be bit overwhelming, you do not have to follow the schedule that is set in this book. Here are some examples of how to alternatively use My Weekly Korean Vocabulary: spend one week going over one day's expressions in detail; go over each keyword and look back at the expressions at a later time; study the shorter phrases first, then tackle the longer ones. Whichever way you choose to study, it is important that you study DAILY. Even if you can only dedicate five minutes a day to studying Korean, studying every day is the best way to make the most out of this book.

The keyword is said aloud a total of four times. Male and female native Korean speakers take turns saying the keyword at a natural, slow, and fast speed. Each of the sample expressions will also be read four times and in the same fashion.

Tracks are labeled in sequential order. For example, Week 1 Days 1-7 are tracks 01-07. Week 2 Day 1 is track 08.

You can download the tracks from the Talk To Me In Korean website by typing in the following link: **https://www.talktomeinkorean.com/audio**.

Procrastinate no more and start studying right now!

The Drawing Project

Share Your Art with the World !

"The Drawing Project" was a collaborative design project which invited listeners and supporters of Talk To Me In Korean to submit drawings that depict the keywords used in My Weekly Korean Vocabulary. The participants were invited to freely choose a word to illustrate based on a given list.

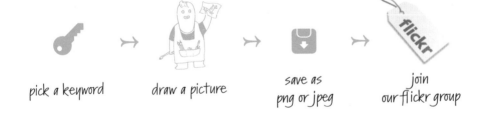

pick a keyword   draw a picture   save as png or jpeg   join our flickr group

The drawings were submitted under the Creative Commons agreement so that any of the artwork created and shared by users for this project can be used freely for any purpose. (CC BY-SA Attribution-Share Alike Creative Commons)

You can download the drawings here: **https://www.flickr.com/groups/thedrawingproject**

What is Open Content?

Open Content is a concept that expands on the existing concept of sourcing: the state where creative content is free for sharing. CCL, or Creative Commons License, is a copyright license that gives others the right to use work freely. Although sharing any type of work openly and freely is not an easy thing to do, many people and companies are already enjoying the benefits. Talk To Me In Korean has used this method since its inception in 2009 to provide materials so that anyone can study Korean.

People whose drawings were selected for this book:

Andrius Repsys	Dana Valle	Hyerin Jeong
Mabeopsa	Bondareva Olga	flyingfi5h
Lilian Phu	Kyung-hwa Sun	Hyunwoo Sun
CCKorea	Seokjin Jin	Mijin Song
Krishna	Jade Calliste-Edgar	Eliza Mária Sándor
Apin Ryuna	Kanari Pictures	Marija Vukosa
Margaret Cartwright	Bae Seunghee	Moonhee Shin
Michelle Smith	Hyojin An	Jenny Bee

Week 1

Day 1   Audio Track : 01
보다 [bo-da]
to see; to look; to watch; to meet up;
to read

Day 2   Audio Track : 02
전화 [jeon-hwa]
phone call; telephone

Day 3   Audio Track : 03
듣다 [deut-tta]
to hear; to listen

Day 4   Audio Track : 04
친구 [chin-gu]
friend

Day 5   Audio Track : 05
말하다 [mal-ha-da]
to talk; to say; to speak; to tell

Day 6   Audio Track : 06
노래 [no-rae]
song

Day 7   Audio Track : 07
가르치다 [ga-reu-chi-da]
to teach

보다

to see; to look; to watch;
to meet up; to read

볼 것
something to see/look/watch

책을 보다
to read a book

책 = book

영화를 보다
to watch a movie

영화 = movie

애를 보다
to babysit

애 = kid, child; baby
애 is the contracted form of 아이.

간을 보다
to taste (to see if the food is too salty or too bland)

간 = saltiness (of food)

자, 여기를 보세요.
Well, look here.

자 = Well (interjection to start a sentence)
여기 = here, this place

이것 좀 보세요.
Look at this.

이것 = this; this thing
좀 = a little; please
-(으)세요 = (polite) imperative

이런 거 처음 봐요.
I have never seen anything like this before.

이런 = N + like this
이런 is the adjective form of 이렇다.
이런 거 = something like this
거 = thing, stuff; object
In the dictionary and in writing, 거 is 것, when spoken, 거 is used for the ease of pronunciation.
처음 = first; for the first time

내일 시험 봐야 돼요.
I have to take a test tomorrow.

내일 = tomorrow
시험 = test, examination
-아/어/여야 되다 = to have to + V

왜 시계를 자꾸 봐요?
Why do you keep looking at your watch?

왜 = why; for what reason; how come
시계 = clock, watch
자꾸 = repeatedly, again and again

이 책 나중에 꼭 볼 거예요.
I will read this book later, definitely.

이 = this   나중에 = later
꼭 = for sure; at any cost; certainly; definitely; make sure to (do something); tight

맛을 보다가 혀를 데었어요.

I burned my tongue while I was tasting the food.

맛 = taste	혀 = tongue
맛을 보다 = to taste	데다 = to burn oneself

어제 친구랑 영화를 봤어요.

Yesterday, I watched a movie with my friend.

어제 = yesterday
친구 = friend

보면 볼수록 마음에 들어요.

The more I see it, the more I like it.

-(으)면 -(으)ㄹ수록 = the more..., the more...
마음 = heart; mind
들다 = to enter; to be categorized as; to be in
마음에 들다 = to like

우리 다음 주에 꼭 한번 봐요.

Let's make sure to meet up next week.

우리 = we; us	다음 = next
주 = week	한번 = one time, once
한번 -아/어/여요 = Let's + V + sometime in the future	

어제 우연히 그 사람을 봤어요.

I saw him by chance yesterday.

우연히 = by chance
그 = the; that
사람 = person, people

너무 어두워서 볼 수가 없었어요.

I couldn't see it because it was too dark.

너무 = too much, excessively; very
어둡다 = to be dark
-아/어/여서 = because, since
-(으)ㄹ 수 없다 = to be unable to + V, can't

보자마자 너무 마음에 들어서
샀어요.

As soon as I saw it, I liked it so much that I bought it.

-자마자 = as soon as + S + V
사다 = to buy

시간이 없어서 아직 그 영화 못 봤어요.

I haven't had time, so I haven't been able to watch that movie yet.

시간 = time; hour	없다 = to not have; to not be there; to not exist
아직 = (not) yet	
못 = can't	

친구가 그 드라마 재미없다고 해서 안 봤
어요.

A friend of mine told me that the drama was not interesting, so I didn't watch it.

드라마 = TV drama, soap opera
-다고 해서 = since someone says/said ...
안 = not
재미없다 = to be not funny; to be not interesting; to be boring

전화

phone call; telephone

ⓒⓕⓞ 마법사

집 전화
home phone

국제 전화
international phone call

장난 전화
prank phone call

전화하다
to call; to telephone

전화를 받다
to receive a call

전화를 걸다
to call someone; to make a phone call

전화를 끊다
to hang up the phone

전화 왔어요.
You have a phone call.

전화 받으세요.
Please pick up the phone.

왜 전화했어요?
Why did you call?

장난 전화였어요.
It was a prank phone call.

집 = house, home

국제 = international

장난 = prank

하다 = to do

받다 = to receive

걸다 = to dial (a phone call); to hang (something)

끊다 = to hang up (a phone); to cut off

오다 = to come

밤에 전화해도 돼요?
Can I call you at night?

밤 = night
-아/어/여도 되다 = to be okay to + V

나중에 전화해 주세요.
Call me later.

-아/어/여 주세요 = (polite) Please do + something + for me

어제 왜 전화 안 했어요?
Why didn't you call me yesterday?

앞으로 전화하지 마세요.
Don't call me ever again.

앞으로 = from now on
-지 마세요 = (polite) Don't + V

전화를 했으면 말을 하세요.
You should say something when you've called someone.

-(으)면 = if + S + V; when/once + S + V
말 = language; what one says; expression; word; term
말을 하다 = to speak; to talk; to tell; to say

전화를 받자마자 끊어졌어요.
As soon as I picked up the phone, it got cut off.

끊어지다 = to be cut off

전화를 걸 때마다 통화중이에요.
Whenever I call, the line is busy.

-(으)ㄹ 때 = when/while + S + V
-(으)ㄹ 때마다 = whenever + S + V
통화중이다 = the line is busy

지금 회의 중이라 전화를 받을 수 없어요.
I am in the middle of a meeting, therefore I can't answer the phone.

지금 = now
회의 = meeting
회의 중 = in the middle of a meeting

국제 전화를 많이 해서 전화비가 많이 나왔어요.
I made a lot of international phone calls, so I received a big phone bill.

많다 = to be a lot
많이 is an adverb form of 많다.
전화비 = phone bill
나오다 = to come out

듣다
to hear; to listen

ⓒ①③ *Lilian Phu*

음악을 듣다
to listen to music

음악 = music

조언을 듣다
to listen to advice

조언 = advice

이야기를 듣다
to listen to a story

이야기 = story; what one says

지금 뭐 듣고 있어요?
What are you listening to now?

뭐 = what; something
뭐 is the contracted form of 무엇.
-고 있다 = to be + V-ing

제 말 좀 들어 보세요.
Listen to my story.
Listen to me.

제 = (polite) my; I
-아/어/여 보다 = to try + V-ing

음악 듣는 거 좋아해요?
Do you like listening to music?

좋아하다 = to like

오디오북을 듣고 있어요.
I'm listening to an audiobook.

오디오북 = audiobook

부모님 말씀 잘 들을게요.
I will listen to (and be obedient to) my parents.

부모님 = parents
말씀 = (honorific) word; advice; what one says
잘 = well; carefully
말(씀)을 듣다 = to obey, do what someone tells
you to do

신나는 음악이 듣고 싶어요.
I want to listen to some exciting music.

신나다 = to be exciting; to be excited
-고 싶다 = to want to + V

이 사람 노래는 못 듣겠어요.
I can't stand this person's songs.

노래 = song

제 이야기 좀 들어 주실래요?
Can you listen to my story?

-아/어/여 주다 = to do something for someone

재미있는 이야기를 들었어요.
I heard a funny story.

재미있다 = to be fun; to be funny; to be
interesting

자기 전에는 조용한 음악을 들어요.

I listen to quiet music before I go to sleep.

자다 = to sleep
-기 전에 = before + V-ing
조용하다 = to be quiet

그 사람 이름은 들어 본 적이 없어요.

I have never heard of his name.

이름 = name
-아/어/여 본 적이 없다 = to have not + p.p.

친구의 조언을 듣고 마음을 바꿨어요.

After I listened to my friend's advice, I've changed my mind.

바꾸다 = to change

그 사람 말을 듣고 있자니 화가 났어요.

I got angry as I listened to his story.

-고 있자니 = as + S + be + V-ing + as a result
화 = anger
화가 나다 = to get angry

이제 와서 그런 말은 듣고 싶지 않아요.

I don't want to hear things like that right now.

이제 와서 = now; now that things have happened like this
그런 = (something) like that; such + noun

그때 엄마 말을 듣지 않은 걸 후회해요.

I regret that I didn't listen to my mom back then.

그때 = at that time; back then
엄마 = mom
후회하다 = to regret

다른 사람의 의견을 듣는 것도 중요해요.

It is important to listen to other people's opinions.

다르다 = to be different
다른 = other; another
의견 = opinion
중요하다 = to be important

저 사람은 항상 듣기 좋은 말만 해서 신뢰가 안 가요.

He is always just saying flattering things, so I can't trust him.

저 = that
항상 = always, all the time
듣다 = to hear; to listen
-기 좋다 = to be easy to + V; to be nice to + V
듣기 좋은 말 = flattery
-만 = only; just
신뢰 = trust
신뢰가 가다 = to be trustworthy

친구
friend

cc①① *Andrius Repsys*

*In Korean, the concept of "친구" is relatively smaller than that of the English word "friend." Typically, the word 친구 refers to someone who is the same age as you. Even if you are close to someone, if that person is older or younger than you, you don't really introduce them as your 친구, instead, kinship terms, such as 언니, 오빠, 누나, and 형 are often used. When you talk about your friends to someone, you can use 아는 in front of the kinship terms to mean "... that I know." For example, if you are a 20-year-old female and your friend is a 21-year-old female, you can introduce her as "아는 언니."

좋은 친구
good friend

좋다 = to be good, likable; to be desirable; to be nice; to like
좋은 is the adjective form of 좋다.

나쁜 친구
bad friend

나쁘다 = to be bad
나쁜 is the adjective form of 나쁘다.

친한 친구
close friend

친하다 = to be close (with other people)
친한 is the adjective form of 친하다.

학교 친구
friend from school

학교 = school

친구랑 놀다
to play with a friend

놀다 = to play; to hang out

친구가 되다
to become friends

되다 = to become

친구를 사귀다
to make a friend

사귀다 = to make friends; to date someone

친구랑 싸우다
to fight with a friend

싸우다 = to fight

제 친구예요.
This is my friend.

친구니까 괜찮아요.
It's okay because we are friends.

괜찮다 = to be okay; to be alright; to be nice

친구를 만날 거예요.
I am going to meet my friend.

만나다 = to meet (up)
-(으)ㄹ 것이다 = will; to be going to + V

친구 추가 해 주세요.
Please add me as a friend.

추가하다 = to add

친구가 선물로 줬어요.
My friend gave it to me as a gift.

선물 = gift, present

친구랑 연락이 끊겼어요.
My friend and I lost touch.

연락 = contact
끊기다 = to be cut off; to be disconnected

친구들한테 물어볼게요.
I'll ask my friend.

물어보다 = to ask
-(으)ㄹ게요 = I promise I will + V; I will + V

어제 친구 집에서 잤어요.
I slept over at my friend's house yesterday.

유학 간 친구가 보고 싶어요.
I miss my friend who has gone to study abroad.

유학 = studying abroad
가다 = to go; to leave

어제 고향 친구들을 만났어요.
Yesterday, I met my friends from my hometown.

고향 = hometown

친구들 중에서 제가 제일 키가 커요.
I'm the tallest among my friends.

중(에서) = among; out of; between; in
제일 = the most + adjective/adverb
키 = height
크다 = to be big; to be tall; to be loud

친구들을 만나면 항상 수다를 떨어요.
Whenever I meet my friends, we always chat.

수다 = chat
수다를 떨다 = to chat

말하다

to talk; to say; to speak;
to tell

© ① ② *Lilian Phu*

짧게 말하다
to make a quick remark

짧다 = to be short
짧게 is an adverb form of 짧다.

생각을 말하다
to voice one's opinion

생각 = thought; opinion; idea

솔직히 말하다
to say honestly

솔직히 = honestly; to be honest

있는 그대로 말하다
to say something as is

있는 그대로 = as is; without changing it

저한테만 말해 보세요.
Just tell me (if you don't want to tell anyone else).

저 = (polite) I; me

아무한테도 말하면 안 돼요.
You shouldn't tell anybody about this.

아무한테도 = to nobody, (not) to anybody
-(으)면 안 되다 = shouldn't; must not

그 사람이 뭐라고 말했어요?
What did he say?

-라고 is a verb ending used for citing or quoting a noun.

지금 말하고 싶은 게 뭐예요?
What is it that you want to say now?

잠깐 기다리라고 말해 주세요.
Please, tell them to wait for a minute.

잠깐 = short time; for a moment
기다리다 = to wait

어떻게 그렇게 말할 수 있어요?
How could you say that?

어떻게 = how
그렇게 = like that; such + adjective/adverb
-(으)ㄹ 수 있다 = to be able to, can; there is a chance that + S + V

조금만 더 크게 말해 주실래요?
Can you speak up a little?

조금 = a little
더 = more
-(으)ㄹ래요? = Do you want to + V?; Shall we + V?

다른 사람이 말하는 걸 들었어요.

I heard other people talking about it.
I heard them talking about it.

10시까지 여기로 오라고 말했어요.

I told them to come here by 10 o'clock.

10시 = ten o'clock

그 사람이랑은 말하고 싶지 않아요.

I don't want to talk with him.

-고 싶지 않다 = to not want to + V

시간이 없으니까 짧게 말해 주세요.

I don't have much time, so please make it short.

-(으)니까 = since, because

제가 어제 뭐라고 말했는지 기억해요?

Do you remember what I said yesterday?

기억하다 = to remember

필요한 게 있으면 뭐든지 말해 주세요.

If you need anything, tell me whatever it may be.

필요하다 = to need; to be necessary
있다 = to be there; to exist; to have
뭐든지 = whatever it is, anything

그 문제에 대해서는 말하고 싶지 않아요.

I don't want to talk about that problem.

문제 = problem; issue; thing; matter
-에 대해서 = about; regarding + N; concerning + N

화내지 않을 테니까 솔직히 말해 주세요.

I won't get angry, so just tell me honestly.

화내다 = to be angry at someone; to yell at someone out of anger

무슨 일이 있었는지 있는 그대로 말할게요.

I will tell you exactly what happened.

무슨 = what; what kind of
일 = work; task; thing, stuff; occasion

노래
song

노래방
karaoke, singing room

노래방 = karaoke, singing room

_____

사랑 노래
love song

사랑 = love

_____

노래 소리
singing; song; sound of music

소리 = sound

_____

신나는 노래
exciting song; cheerful song

신나는 is the adjective form of 신나다.

_____

노래를 듣다
to listen to a song

_____

노래를 부르다
to sing a song

부르다 = to call (one's name); to sing

_____

노래를 못하다
to be not good at singing

노래를 하다 = to sing

_____

노래를 흥얼거리다
to hum

흥얼거리다 = to hum

_____

노래방 갈래요?
Do you want to go to karaoke?

-(으)ㄹ래요? = Do you want to + V?

_____

이 노래 제목 알아요?
Do you know the title of this song?

제목 = title
알다 = to know

_____

이 노래 좋은 것 같아요.
I think this song is good.

- 것 같다 = It seems/looks like + S + V

노래 소리 좀 키워 주세요.
Please turn the music volume up.

키우다 = to raise
소리를 키우다 = to turn up the volume

노래 부르는 거 좋아하세요?
Do you like singing?

신나는 노래 좀 추천해 주세요.
Please recommend some cheerful songs.

추천하다 = to recommend

그 사람은 노래를 정말 잘해요.
He sings very well.

정말 = really; very
잘하다 = to be good at something

그 가수는 춤은 잘 추지만 노래는 잘
못해요.
He dances really well, but can't sing well.

가수 = singer
춤 = dance
추다 = to dance

학교 가는 길에 버스에서 항상 노래를 들
어요.
I always listen to songs on the bus on my way to school.

길 = road, street; way
- 가는 길 = on one's way to + place
버스 = bus

저는 노래를 정말 못하니까 노래
시키지 마세요.
I really can't sing, so don't make me sing.

시키다 = to make someone + V

기분이 좋아서 저도 모르게 노래를
흥얼거렸어요.
I felt so happy that I was humming without even noticing
it.

기분 = feelings; mood
모르게 = without knowing; without meaning
to + V

저는 노래는 잘 못 부르지만 노래방에서
노래를 부르는 거는 좋아해요.
I can't sing very well, but I do like singing at karaoke.

가르치다

to teach

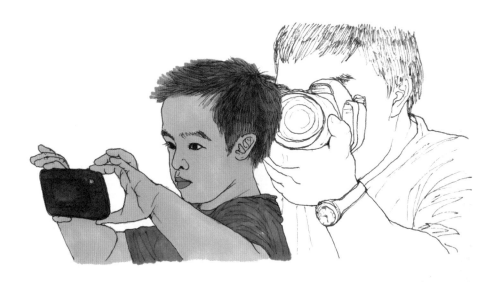

ⓒⓑⓞ 마법사

가르쳐 주다
to teach; to tell

영어를 가르치다
to teach English

영어 = the English language

길을 가르쳐 주다
to show the way

테니스를 가르치다
to teach tennis

테니스 = tennis

연락처를 가르쳐 주다
to tell (someone) the contact number

연락처 = contact; phone number

저 중국어 좀 가르쳐 주세요
Please teach me Chinese.

중국어 = the Chinese language

저는 중학교에서 영어를 가르쳐요.
I teach English in a middle school.

중학교 = middle school

제가 아까 가르쳐 준 거 벌써 잊었어요?

I taught it to you earlier, (and) you've already forgotten?

아까 = before, earlier
벌써 = already
잊다 = to forget

엄마가 요리하는 법을 가르쳐 주셨어요.
My mom taught me how to cook.

요리하다 = to cook
-는 법 = how to + V

저는 한번도 남을 가르쳐 본 적이 없어요.
I have not taught anyone, not even once.

한번도 = (not even) once
남 = other people, others

이거 이해가 잘 안 되는데, 좀 가르쳐 주세요.
I don't understand this well, (so) please teach me.

이거 = this thing; this
이해가 되다 = to be able to understand

친구가 길을 잘못 가르쳐 줘서 길을 잃었어요.

My friend told me the wrong way, so I got lost.

잘못 = in the wrong way
길을 잃다 = to lose one's way; to get lost

남을 가르치는 일이 쉬운 일은 아닌 것 같아요.

I think teaching other people is not easy.

쉽다 = to be easy
쉬운 is the adjective form of 쉽다.
아니다 = to be not

그 사람 핸드폰 번호 알면 저 좀 가르쳐 주세요.

If you know the person's number, please tell me.

그 사람 = that person; he, she
핸드폰 = mobile phone
번호 = number

이 서점에 가고 싶은데 어떻게 가는지 가르쳐 주세요.

I want to go to this bookstore, (so) please tell me how to go there.

서점 = bookstore

어제는 엄마에게 스마트 폰 사용법을 가르쳐 드렸어요.

I taught my mom how to use a smartphone yesterday.

스마트 폰 = smartphone
사용법 = how to use + N
-아/어/여 드리다 = (honorific) to do something for someone

주말에는 아빠가 운전을 가르쳐 주시기로 약속했어요.

My dad promised to teach me to drive during the weekend.

주말 = weekend   아빠 = dad
운전 = driving
-기로 약속하다 = to promise to + V
-아/어/여 주시다 = (honorific) someone does something for me/us (usually a positive thing)

저는 저희 아이들에게 거짓말을 하면 안 된다고 가르쳤어요.

I taught my children that they must not tell lies.

저희 = (polite) we, us; our
아이 = child, kid; baby
거짓말을 하다 = to lie

어제 친구가 어떻게 하는지 가르쳐 줬는데 벌써 잊어버렸어요.

My friend showed me how to do it yesterday, but I already forgot.

잊어버리다 = to forget

제 꿈은 학교 선생님이 되어서 학생들에게 음악을 가르치는 거예요.

My dream is to become a school teacher and teach music to students.

꿈 = dream
선생님 = teacher
학생 = student

Week 2

먹다
to eat; to drink

먹을 것
something to eat; food

밥을 먹다.
to eat something; to have a meal

밥 먹었어요.
I ate.

뭐 먹었어요?
What did you eat?

뭐 먹고 싶어요?
What do you want to eat?

같이 밥 먹어요.
Let's eat together.

밥 먹으러 가요.
Let's go eat.

이거 먹어도 돼요?
Can I eat this?

누가 다 먹었어요?
Who ate all of this?

아무도 안 먹어요?
Nobody wants to eat?

먹을 것 좀 주세요.
Please give me something to eat.

것 = thing, stuff; object
먹을 것 literally means "thing to eat," but it is often used as a set expression that refers to food in general.

밥 = food; meal; cooked rice

뭐 = what; something
뭐 is the contracted form of 무엇.

-고 싶다 = to want to + V

같이 = together; with + N

-(으)러 가다 = to go to + V

이거 = this thing; this
-아/어/여도 되다 = to be okay to + V

누가 = who; someone (subject)
누가 is the subject form of 누구.
다 = all; every (thing)

아무도 = nobody; anybody (always used with a negative sentence structure)
안 = not

좀 = a little; please
주다 = to give
-(으)세요 = (polite) imperative

먹을 거 사러 왔어요.
I came here to buy something to eat.

먹을 거 = food (the same as 먹을 것)
사다 = to buy
-(으)러 오다 = to come to + V

매운 거 잘 못 먹어요.
I can't eat spicy food that well.

맵다 = to be spicy; to be hot
매운 is the adjective form of 맵다
거 = thing, stuff; object (the same as 것)
잘 = well; carefully
못 = can't

먹자마자 잠들었어요.
I fell asleep as soon as I ate.

-자마자 = as soon as + S + V
잠들다 = to fall asleep

집에 먹을 것이 없어요.
There is nothing to eat at home.

집 = house, home
없다 = to not have; to not be there; to not exist

배불러서 먹고 싶지 않아요.
I'm full, so I don't want to eat.

배 부르다 = one feels full
-고 싶지 않다 = to not want to + V

너무 많이 먹어서 배가 불러요.
I ate too much, so I'm full.

너무 = too much, excessively; very
많다 = to be a lot
많이 is an adverb form of 많다.
배 = stomach, belly

내일은 친구랑 저녁을 먹을 거예요.
Tomorrow I am going to eat dinner with my friend.

내일 = tomorrow
친구 = friend
저녁 = evening; dinner
-(으)ㄹ 것이다 = will; to be going to + V

먹는 음식 가지고 장난치지 마세요.
Don't play with your food.

음식 = food
먹는 음식 is a commonly used set expression that refers to food.
가지고 = with; using
장난치다 = to play with something; to play a trick/prank
-지 마세요 = (polite) Don't + V

너무 맛이 없어서 먹을 수가 없어요.
It tastes really bad, so I can't eat it.

맛 = taste
맛이 없다 = to be not tasty; to taste bad
-(으)ㄹ 수 없다 = to be unable to + V, can't

공부

studies, one's learning

영어 공부
English studies

영어 = the English language

공부 방법
study method

방법 = method, way

한국어 공부
studying Korean

한국어 = the Korean language

공부할 시간
time for studying

-(으)ㄹ 시간 = time to + V; time for + V-ing

공부하다
to study

하다 = to do

공부를 잘하다
to be good at studying; to have good grades in school

잘하다 = to be good at something

공부를 못하다
to be bad at studying; to have bad grades in school

못하다 = to be bad/poor at something

요즘 뭐 공부하세요?
What are you studying these days?

요즘 = these days, lately

공부할 게 너무 많아요.
I have too much to study.

-(으)ㄹ 게 = to + V (subject)
-(으)ㄹ 게 is the contracted form of -(으)ㄹ 것이.

시끄러워서 공부가 안 돼요.
Since it's noisy here, I can't study.

시끄럽다 = to be noisy, loud
-아/어/여서 = because, since
안 되다 = S + doesn't work; can't + V

공부할 시간이 너무 부족해요.
I don't have enough time to study.

부족하다 = to be insufficient; to not have enough + N

공부는 해도 해도 끝이 없어요.
No matter how much you study, there's always more (to study).

-아/어/여도 = even though; no matter how much + S + V
끝 = end, finish
끝이 없다 = there is no end; to never end

혼자 공부하면 포기하기 쉬워요.
If you study alone, it's easy to give up.

혼자 = alone, by oneself
-(으)면 = if + S + V; when/once + S + V
포기하다 = to give up
-기 쉽다 = to be easy to + V

이 책은 공부에 도움이 많이 돼요.
This book helps a lot with studying.

이 = this
책 = book
도움 = help
도움이 되다 = to be helpful

저는 학교 다닐 때 공부를 못했어요.
When I was going to school, I was not a good student.

저 = (polite) I; me
학교 = school
다니다 = to go to (a place); to attend
-(으)ㄹ 때 = when/while + S + V

그 사람은 외국에서 공부하고 왔어요.
He studied abroad (and returned).

그 = the; that
외국 = foreign country
-고 오다 = to go do something and then come back

엄마가 방에 들어와서 공부하는 척 했어요.
My mom came into my room, so I pretended to be studying.

엄마 = mom
방 = room
들어오다 = to come in
- 척 하다 = to pretend

어제 공부한 내용이 하나도 기억이 안 나요.
I can't remember anything I studied yesterday.

어제 = yesterday
내용 = content; material
하나 = one (native Korean number)
하나도 = not even one; not at all
기억 = memory
기억이 나다 = to remember

한국어는 공부하면 공부할수록 재미있어요.
The more you study the Korean language, the more fun it is.

-(으)면 -(으)ㄹ수록 = the more ..., the more ....
재미있다 = to be fun; to be funny; to be interesting

어제 밤을 새워서 공부했더니 너무 피곤해요.
I stayed up all night studying, so I am really exhausted.

밤 = night
밤을 새우다 = to stay up all night
-았/었/였더니 = since/because + I/we + V-ed
피곤하다 = to be tired, exhausted; to be tiring

마시다

to drink

Margaret Cartwright

마실 것
something to drink; beverage

술을 마시다
to drink alcohol

술 = alcohol

물을 마시다
to drink water

물 = water

뭐 마실래요?
What do you want to drink?

저는 녹차 마실래요.
I want to drink green tea.

녹차 = green tea

저는 술을 못 마셔요.
I can't drink alcohol.

저는 커피 안 마셔요.
I don't drink coffee.

커피 = coffee

마실 것 좀 드릴까요?
Shall I give you something to drink?

드리다 = (honorific) to give

이거 한번 마셔 보세요.
Try drinking this.

한번 -아/어/여 보다 = to try + V-ing

마실 것 좀 사다 주세요.
Go and buy me something to drink.

사다 주다 = to buy something for someone and bring it to that person

목이 말라서 물을 마셨어요.
I was thirsty, so I drank water.

목 = throat; neck
마르다 = to dry; to be dried
목이 마르다 = to be thirsty

My Weekly Korean Vocabulary Book 1

와인 마시는 거 좋아하세요?
Do you like drinking wine?

와인 = wine
좋아하다 = to like

저는 아침마다 커피를 마셔요.
I drink coffee every morning.

아침 = morning; breakfast
-마다 = every + N

콜라를 마시면 기분이 좋아져요.
Drinking cola makes me feel happy.

콜라 = cola
기분 = feelings; mood
좋다 = to be good, likable; to be desirable; to be nice; to like
-아/어/여지다 = to become + adjective

오늘은 커피를 세 잔이나 마셨어요.
Today, I drank as many as three cups of coffee.

오늘 = today
잔 = counter for glasses, cups, or shots
-이나 = as many as + number, as much as + amount

어젯밤에 술을 너무 많이 마셨어요.
Last night, I drank too much alcohol.

어젯밤 = last night

삼겹살을 먹을 때는 소주가 마시고 싶어져요.
When I eat samgyeopsal, I feel like drinking soju.

삼겹살 = pork belly meat
소주 = soju

너무 추워서 따뜻한 음료수가 마시고 싶어요.
It is really cold, so I want to drink a hot beverage.

춥다 = to be cold
따뜻하다 = to be warm
따뜻한 is the adjective form of 따뜻하다.
음료수 = beverage

오늘 저녁에 친구하고 맥주 마시러 갈 거예요.
This evening, I am going to go drink beer with my friend.

-하고 = with + N
맥주 = beer

불이 났을 때는 연기를 마시지 않도록 주의해야 해요.
When there's a fire, you have to be careful to not inhale the smoke.

불 = fire
불이 나다 = to have a fire; a fire breaks out
연기 = smoke
-지 않도록 = not to + V
주의하다 = to be careful (to/not to + V)
-아/어/여야 하다 = should; have to; must

일
work; task

할 일
work to do; something to do

집안일
housework

안 = in; inside

힘든 일
difficult work; exhausting work

힘들다 = to be difficult, hard, tough; to have a
hard time; to be tiring; to be tired
힘든 is the adjective form of 힘들다.

지루한 일
boring work; tedious work

지루하다 = to be boring; to be bored
지루한 is the adjective form of 지루하다.

일이 많다
to have a lot of work

일이 없다
to have no work

일을 하다
to work

일을 잘하다
to do work well

일을 맡기다
to leave work to (someone)
to entrust (someone) with a task

맡기다 = to leave something to someone; to
entrust

일 다 했어요?
Did you finish everything?
Have you finished working?

어떤 일 하세요?
What kind of work do you do?

어떤 = what kind of; which

그 사람은 일을 너무 못해요.

He really does not do work well.
He is really bad at his job.

그 사람 = that person; he, she

그 사람은 일을 아주 열심히 해요.

He works really hard.

아주 = very, really
열심히 = (to do something) hard, diligently

오늘 할 일을 내일로 미루지 마세요.

Don't put off until tomorrow what you should do today.

미루다 = to delay, postpone, put off

회사 일이 너무 힘들어서 회사를 그만뒀어요.

I quit the company because the company work was too exhausting.

회사 = company; office
그만두다 = to quit

할 일이 너무 많아서 지금은 나갈 수가 없어요.

I have too much work to do, so I cannot go out right now.

지금 = now
나가다 = to go out
-(으)ㄹ 수(가) 없다 = to be not able to + V; can't

지금 많이 안 바쁘면 제 일 좀 도와줄 수 있어요?

If you are not that busy right now, can you help me with my work?

바쁘다 = to be busy
제 = (polite) my; I
도와주다 = to help, give a hand
-(으)ㄹ 수 있다 = can, to be able to; there is a chance that + S + V

오늘은 회사에 일이 많아서 야근을 해야 할 것 같아요.

I think I have to work overtime today because there is a lot of work (to be done) at the company.

야근 = working overtime
야근을 하다 = to work overtime
-(으)ㄹ 것 같다 = I think + S + will/be going to; it seems like + S + will/be going to

요즘 일이 너무 바빠서 제대로 잠을 잘 시간도 없어요.

I am so busy with work these days that I don't even have time to sleep properly.

제대로 = properly
잠을 자다 = to sleep
시간 = time; hour

일을 열심히 하는 것도 중요하지만 건강도 챙기셔야죠.

Working hard is important as well, but you should also take care of your health.

중요하다 = to be important
-지만 = but, however; though
건강 = one's health
챙기다 = to take care of; to pack, take; to gather all together

읽다
to read

읽을거리
reading material; something to read

책을 읽다
to read a book

신문을 읽다
to read a newspaper

신문 = newspaper

큰 소리로 읽다
to read loudly; to read out loud

크다 = to be big; to be tall; to be loud
큰 is the adjective form of 크다.
소리 = sound

이 책 읽어 보셨어요?
Have you read this book?

이 = this
-아/어/여 보다 = to try + V-ing

그 기사 읽어 봤어요?
Did you read that article?

기사 = article

뭔가 읽을거리 없나요?
Is there anything to read?

뭔가 = something (subject)
뭔가 is the contracted form of 무언가.
읽을거리 = reading material, something to read

큰 소리로 읽어 보세요.
Read out loud, please.

이 잡지 읽어도 되나요?
Can I read this magazine?

저는 한자를 읽을 줄 몰라요.
I don't know how to read Chinese characters.

한자 = Korean name for Chinese characters
-(으)ㄹ 줄 모르다 = to not know how to + V

저는 책을 읽으면 잠이 와요.
I feel sleepy when I read a book.

잠이 오다 = to be sleepy; to feel drowsy

제가 빌려준 책 다 읽으셨어요?
Have you finished reading the book I lent you?

빌려주다 = to lend
다 + verb = to finish + V-ing

주말 동안에 이 책을 다 읽었어요.
I finished this book over the weekend.

주말 = weekend
동안 = during, while; for + period of time

그 책 다 읽으면 저 좀 빌려주세요.
When you finish the book, please lend it to me.

이 잡지는 재미가 없어서 읽기 싫어요.
This magazine is not interesting, so I don't want to read it.

잡지 = magazine
재미가 없다 = to be not fun; to be not funny; to be not interesting; to be boring
-기 싫다 = to not feel like + V-ing; to not like + V-ing; to not want to + V

어제 책을 읽느라고 밤에 늦게 잤어요.
I went to bed late last night because I was reading a book.

-느라고 = because + S + was V-ing
늦다 = to be late
늦게 is the adverb form of 늦다.
자다 = to sleep

한글을 읽을 줄은 아는데 쓸 줄은 몰라요.
I know how to read Hangeul, but I don't know how to write it.

한글 = Hangeul (Korean alphabet)
-(으)ㄹ 줄 알다 = to know how to + V
쓰다 = to write

과제 때문에 읽어야 할 책을 아직 안 읽었어요.
Reading that book is my assignment, but I haven't read it yet.

과제 = homework; assignment
때문에 = because (of), since
아직 = (not) yet

이 책은 어린이들이 읽기에는 어려운 것 같아요.
I think this book is difficult for children to read.

어린이 = kid, child
-기에 = (to be too + adjective) + to + V
어렵다 = to be difficult
어려운 is the adjective form of 어렵다.
- 것 같다 = It seems/looks like + S + V

그 책 너무 재미있어서 하루만에 다 읽었어요.
The book is so interesting that I finished reading it in only one day.

하루 = one day
-만 = only; just

질문
question

ⓒⓘⓞ 마법사

이상한 질문
weird question

이상하다 = to be weird, odd, strange
이상한 is the adjective form of 이상하다.

어려운 질문
difficult question

난처한 질문
awkward question

난처하다 = to be in an awkward situation
난처한 is the adjective form of 난처하다.

날카로운 질문
sharp question; penetrating question

날카롭다 = to be sharp; to be penetrating
날카로운 is the adjective form of 날카롭다.

바보같은 질문
stupid question

바보같다 = to be stupid, foolish
바보같은 is the adjective form of 바보같다.

개인적인 질문
personal question

개인적이다 = to be personal, private
개인적인 is the adjective form of 개인적이다.

질문하다
to ask a question

질문에 대답하다
to answer a question

대답하다 = to answer

질문 있어요.
I have a question.

있다 = to be there; to exist; to have

질문 있나요?
Do you have any questions?

질문 하나 해도 될까요?
May I ask a question?

하나 = one (native Korean number)
-아/어/여도 될까요? = (polite) Can + S + V?

질문이 좀 이상한 것 같아요.
I think the question is a little bit strange.

먼저 제 질문에 답해 주세요.
Please answer my question first.

먼저 = first; before + N
-아/어/여 주세요 = (polite) Please do + something + for me

대답하기 참 어려운 질문이네요.
It's such a difficult question to answer.

참 = very, quite
-(으)네요 is a sentence ending that expresses realization of a fact or agreement to a statement.

그 질문에는 대답하고 싶지 않네요.
I don't want to answer that question.

개인적인 질문은 하지 말아 주세요.
Please don't ask any personal questions.

질문을 하다 = to ask a question
-지 말아 주세요 = Please don't + V.

질문이 있으면 손을 들어 주세요.
If you have any questions, please raise your hand.

손 = hand
들다 = to raise; to pick (something) up

질문은 발표가 끝난 다음에 받겠습니다.
We will take questions after the presentation is finished.

발표 = presentation
끝나다 = to end; to be over
다음에 = next time; later
받다 = to receive

그 질문은 나중에 개인적으로 대답할게요.
I will answer that question later in private.

나중에 = next time; later
-(으)ㄹ게요 = I promise I will + V; I will + V

모르는 게 있으면 바로바로 질문해 주세요.
If you have something that you don't know, please ask me immediately.

모르다 = to not know
바로바로 = immediately

쓰다
to write

글을 쓰다
to write

글 = writing

편지를 쓰다
to write a letter

편지 = letter

소설을 쓰다
to write a novel

소설 = novel, fiction

이메일을 쓰다
to write an e-mail

이메일 = e-mail

뭐라고 썼어요?
What did you write?

-라고 is a verb ending used for citing or quoting a noun.

쓸 말이 없어요.
I have nothing to write.

말 = language; what one says; expression; word; term

언제 쓸 거예요?
When are you going to write it?

언제 = when

이름 좀 써 주세요.
Please write your name.

이름 = name

이름 어떻게 써요?
How do you write your name?

어떻게 = how

이거 누가 썼어요?
Who wrote this?

다 쓰면 보여주세요.
When you finish writing, show it to me.

보여주다 = to show, display

여기에 쓰면 되나요?
Do you want me to write it here?

여기 = here, this place
-(으)면 되다 = to be just supposed to + V; to just have to + V; can just + V

제가 쓴 거 봐 주세요.
Please take a look at what I have written.

처음부터 다시 쓰세요.
Write it all over again from the beginning.

처음 = first; for the first time
다시 = again

이거 영어로 써 주세요.
Write this in English.

영어로 = in English

보고서를 쓰는 중이에요.
I am in the middle of writing a report.

보고서 = report
중이다 = to be V-ing; to be between/middle/in the middle of + V-ing

편지 누구한테 써야 돼요?
To whom should I write this letter?

누구 = who
-아/어/여야 되다 = to have to + V

제가 쓴 이메일 보셨어요?
Did you read the e-mail I wrote to you?

보다 = to see; to look; to watch; to meet up; to read

최근에 편지 쓴 적 있어요?
Have you written a letter recently?

최근에 = recently, lately
-(으)ㄴ 적이 있다 = to have done something

그 사람이 쓴 책은 재미있어요.
The book he wrote is interesting.

그 = that, the
사람 = person
책 = book
재미있다 = to be interesting

Week 3

빠르다
to be fast

빨리 먹다
to eat fast

먹다 = to eat; to drink

말이 빠르다
to have a fast way of talking; to speak fast

말 = language; what one says; expression; word; term

눈치가 빠르다
to have a quick sense of what is happening
to have a fast intuition

눈치 = intuition; quick sense; perceptiveness

걸음이 빠르다
to have a fast walking pace
to walk fast

걸음 = step; (walking) pace

시간이 너무 빨라요.
Time goes too fast.

시간 = time; hour
너무 = too much, excessively; very

제 말이 너무 빠른가요?
Are my words too fast?
Am I speaking too fast?

제 = (polite) my; I

왜 그렇게 밥을 빨리 먹어요?
Why are you eating your meal so quickly?

왜 = why; for what reason; how come
그렇게 = like that; such + adjective/adverb
밥 = food; meal; cooked rice

친구들이 제 걸음이 빠르대요.
My friends tell me I have a fast (walking) pace.
My friends tell me I walk fast.

친구 = friend
-들 is a suffix used to indicate plural.
-대요 = I heard that + S + V; They say + S + V

저 곧 가야 되니까 빨리 주세요.
I have to go soon, so hurry and give it (to me).

저 = (polite) I; me
곧 = soon
가다 = to go; to leave
-아/어/여야 되다 = to have to + V
-(으)니까 = since, because
주다 = to give
-(으)세요 = (polite) imperative

우리 이거 빨리 끝내고 놀러 가요.
Let's finish this quickly and go hang out.

우리 = we; us
이거 = this thing; this
끝내다 = to finish; to get + N + done
놀러 가다 = to go on a trip; to hang out; to visit
-아/어/여요 = imperative; Let's + V

빠르다고 다 좋은 것은 아니에요.
Just because it is fast doesn't mean it's good.

-다고 = just because; saying that S + V
다 = all; every (thing)
좋다 = to be good, likable; to be desirable; to be nice; to like
아니다 = to be not

여기 인터넷 속도 진짜 빠르네요.
The speed of the Internet here is really fast.

여기 = here, this place
인터넷 = the Internet
속도 = speed; pace

-(으)네요 is a sentence ending that expresses realization of a fact or agreement to a statement.

빨리 끝내 주시면 좋을 것 같아요.
It would be good if you get it done quickly.

-아/어/여 주다 = to do something for someone
-(으)면 = if + S + V; when/once + S + V
-(으)ㄹ 것 같다 = I think + S + will/be going to; it seems like + S + will/be going to

어느 길로 가는 게 제일 빠를까요?
Which way will be the fastest?

어느 = which; some
길 = road, street; way
제일 = the best; the most

저 지금 시간 없으니까 빨리 말해요.
I don't have time right now, so talk fast.

지금 = now
없다 = to not have; to not be there; to not exist
말하다 = to talk; to say; to speak; to tell

이 책을 보면 이해가 빨리 될 거예요.
If you read this book, you will quickly understand.

이 = this   책 = book
보다 = to see; to look; to watch; to meet up; to read
책을 보다 = to look at a book; to read a book
이해 = understanding
이해가 되다 = can understand; something makes sense
-(으)ㄹ 것이다 = will; to be going to + V

그 사람은 말이 빨라서 알아듣기 힘들어요.
That person speaks so fast that it's hard to understand.

그 사람 = that person; he, she
알아듣다 = to understand what one says
-기 힘들다 = to be difficult/hard to + V

제일 빨리 가려면 지하철을 타야 될 것 같아요.
To get there quickly, I think we should take the subway.

-(으)려면 = in order to + V
지하철 = subway
타다 = to ride; to get on; to take (vehicle)

그런 일이 있었으면 빨리 저한테 이야기를 했었어야죠.

If there was an incident like that, you should have told me promptly.

그런 = (something) like that; such + noun
일 = work; task; thing, stuff; occasion
있다 = to be there; to exist; to have
이야기 = story; what one says
이야기를 하다 = to talk, speak, say, tell; to have a conversation; to tell a story
-았/었/였어야죠 = you should have + p.p.

버스가 너무 빨리 달려서 버스에 서 있다가 넘어질 뻔했어요.

Since the bus (I was riding) was going so fast, I nearly fell over while standing.

버스 = bus
달리다 = to run
-아/어/여서 = because, since
서 있다 = to be standing
-다가 = as a result of + V-ing
넘어지다 = to fall (down); to trip
-(으)ㄹ 뻔하다 = to almost + V

지각

being late (for school/work/appointment)

©①② *Dana Valle*

지각생
tardy student

지각하다
to be late

_____

학교에 지각하다
to be late for school

학교 = school
지각하다 = to be late

_____

회사에 지각하다
to be late for work

회사 = company; office

_____

또 지각이네요.
You are late again.

또 = again

_____

지각하지 마세요.
Don't be late.

-지 마세요 = (polite) Don't + V

_____

오늘 왜 지각했어요?
Why were you late today?

오늘 = today

_____

오늘 지각할 것 같아요.
I think I will be late today.

_____

그 사람은 맨날 지각해요.
He is always late.

맨날 = every day; all the time

_____

면접에 절대 지각하면 안 돼요.
You should never be late for your job interview.

면접 = (job) interview
절대 = never
-(으)면 안 되다 = shouldn't; must not

_____

오늘은 절대 지각하면 안 돼요.
You must not be late today.

_____

어떻게 오늘 같은 날 지각할 수 있어요?
How could you be late on a day like today?

어떻게 + -(으)ㄹ 수가 있어요? = How could you + V?; How dare you + V?
N + 같은 날 = a day like + N
-(으)ㄹ 수 있다 = can, to be able to; there is a chance that + S + V

오늘은 늦잠을 자서 학교에 지각했어요.
I overslept today and was late for school.

늦잠을 자다 = to get up late, oversleep, sleep in

오늘 아침에는 차가 막혀서 지각을 했어요.
I was late this morning because of traffic.

아침 = morning; breakfast
차가 막히다 = the traffic is bad; the road is jammed with traffic

저는 이번 달에 벌써 세 번이나 지각했어요.
I have already been late (for work/school) three times this month.

이번 = this; this time
달 = month
벌써 = already
세 번 = three times

-이나 = as many as + number, as much as + amount

다섯 번 지각하면 한 번 결석한 것과 똑같아요.
Being late five times is counted as one absence.

다섯 번 = five times
한 번 = once, one time
결석하다 = to be absent; to not go to a class/school
똑같다 = to be the same; to be equal

친구랑 만나기로 했는데 30분이나 지각했어요.
I arranged to meet my friend, but I was 30 minutes late.

친구 = friend
만나다 = to meet (up)
-기로 하다 = to plan to + V; to decide to + V; to make a promise to + V
분 = minute

택시를 타고 회사에 갔는데도 10분 지각했어요.
Even though I went to work by taxi, I was 10 minutes late.

택시 = cab, taxi
-데도 = even though, although

저는 학교 다닐 때 한 번도 지각을 한 적이 없어요.
When I was in school, I was never late (for school).

다니다 = to go to (a place); to attend
-(으)ㄹ 때 = when/while + S + V
한 번도 - 없다 = haven not + V + even once
-(으)ㄴ 적 없다 = to have never p.p.

내일은 중요한 시험이 있으니까 지각하면 안 돼요.
There is an important exam tomorrow, so you can't be late.

내일 = tomorrow
중요하다 = to be important
중요한 is the adjective form of 중요하다.
시험 = test, exam

느리다
to be slow

느린 노래
slow song

노래 = song

말이 느리다
(someone) speaks slowly

걸음이 느리다
(someone) walks slowly

반응이 느리다
one's reaction is slow

반응 = one's reaction

이해가 느리다
to be slow at understanding

동작이 느리다
to act slowly

동작 = one's action

한 박자 느리다
one beat behind in responding or understanding
a little slow in responding or understanding
a little slow on the uptake

하나 = one (native Korean number)
한 is the adjective form of 하나.
박자 = tempo

왜 그렇게 반응이 느려요?
Why is your reaction so slow?

윤아 씨는 말이 정말 느려요.
Yoona speaks very slowly.

석진 씨는 이해가 좀 느려요.
Seokjin is a little slow in understanding.

좀 = a little; please

인터넷이 너무 느려서 짜증나요.
The Internet is really slow and I'm really annoyed.

짜증나다 = to be annoying; to be annoyed

컴퓨터가 너무 느려서 일을 하기 힘들어요.

The computer is so slow that it's hard to work (with it).

컴퓨터 = computer
일을 하다 = to work

앞 차가 너무 느리게 가서 추월해 버렸어요.

The car in front of me was driving really slow, so I passed it.

앞 = in front of; front
차 = car
추월하다 = to pass (a car)
-아/어/여 버리다 is used when talking about something that happened against your hope or expectations.

KTX가 아무리 빨라도 비행기보다는 느려요.

No matter how fast KTX is, it's slower than an airplane.

KTX = Korean Train eXpress
The fastest train running in Korea. Top speed for trains in regular service is currently 305 km/h (190 mph).
아무리 = no matter + adjective/adverb
빠르다 = to be fast
-아/어/여도 = even though; no matter how much + S + V
비행기 = airplane
-보다 = than + N

컴퓨터가 많이 느리면 메모리를 추가하세요.

If your computer is too slow, add memory.

많다 = to be a lot
많이 is the adverb form of 많다.
메모리 = (computer) memory
추가하다 = to add

핸드폰을 4년 동안 썼더니 이제 많이 느려요.

I've been using my mobile phone for four years now, so it's really slow.

핸드폰 = mobile phone
4년 = four years
동안 = during, while; for + period of time
쓰다 = to use; to spend (+ money)
-았/었/였더니 = since/because + I/we + V-ed
이제 = now

저는 겨울에는 이런 느린 노래를 듣는 걸 좋아해요.

I like listening to slow songs like this in the winter.

겨울 = winter
이런 = N + like this
듣다 = to hear; to listen
좋아하다 = to like

저는 걸음이 많이 느려서 어디 갈 때면 집에서 일찍 출발해요.

I walk very slowly whenever I go somewhere, so I leave the house early.

어디 = where; somewhere
-(으)ㄹ 때면 = whenever + S + V
집 = house, home
일찍 = early; soon
출발하다 = to depart

일본어를 배운 지 1주일 밖에 안 돼서 아직 일본어 읽는 속도가 많이 느려요.

It's only been a week since I started learning Japanese, therefore I'm still slow at reading it.

일본어 = the Japanese language
배우다 = to learn; to study
-(으)ㄴ 지 = (to have been a certain amount of time) since + S + V
1주일 = one week
밖에 = just, only
안 = not
~ 밖에 안 되다 = It's only been + (time); It's only been + (time) + since ...
아직 = (not) yet
읽다 = to read

저는 밥 먹는 속도가 느려서 남들이 밥 먹으면서 대화를 할 때 저는 조용히 먹기만 해요.

I eat slowly, so when people have a conversation while eating, I just eat quietly.

남 = other people, others
-(으)면서 = while + S + V-ing
대화 = conversation
대화를 하다 = to have a conversation; to talk
조용하다 = to be quiet
조용히 is an adverb form of 조용하다.
-기만 하다 = just + V; to only + V

요리

cooking, cookery

© ⓘ ◎ *Bondareva Olga*

요리사
cook, chef

요리 책
recipe book, cookbook

요리 재료
ingredients of the dish

재료 = ingredient

요리 학원
cooking school

학원 = private educational institute

요리 솜씨
cooking skill

솜씨 = skill; ability

요리 기구
cooking utensil

기구 = tool

요리 잘하세요?
Are you good at cooking?

잘하다 = to be good at something

저는 요리를 잘 못해요.
I'm not very good at cooking.

잘 = well; carefully
요리를 하다 = to cook
못하다 = to be bad at something; to be poor at something

할 줄 아는 요리 있어요?
Are there any dishes you can cook?

-(으)ㄹ 줄 알다 = to know how to + V

저는 요리에 관심이 많아요.
I'm really interested in cooking.

관심 = interest
관심이 많다 = to be interested in + N + very much

요리 책 보고 따라해 봤어요.
I've tried following the cookbook.

요리 책 = recipe book, cookbook
따라하다 = to copy (someone); to imitate; to mimic
-아/어/여 보다 = to try + V-ing

저는 유명한 요리사가 되고 싶어요.
I want to be a famous chef.

유명하다 = to be famous
유명한 is the adjective form of 유명하다.
요리사 = chef, cook
되다 = to become
-고 싶다 = to want to + V

요즘 요리에 부쩍 재미를 붙였어요.
These days, I've suddeny taken an interest in cooking.

요즘 = these days, lately
부쩍 = (something changed) remarkably; suddenly

재미 = fun
재미를 붙이다 = to become interested in, take an interest in

저희 어머니는 요리를 참 잘하세요.
My mother is very good at cooking.

저희 = (polite) we; us; our
어머니 = mother
참 = very, quite

드디어 한식 요리사 자격증을 땄어요.
I finally got a certificate for Korean cuisine.

드디어 = finally
한식 = Korean food, Korean cuisine
자격증 = certificate
자격증을 따다 = to get a certificate

요리를 할 때는 항상 불을 조심해야 돼요.
When you cook, you always have to be careful with fire.

항상 = always, all the time
불 = fire
조심하다 = to be careful

오랜만에 제 요리 실력을 발휘해 봤어요.

It's been a while since I've showed off my cooking skills.

오랜만에 = first time in a long period of time
발휘하다 = to demonstrate/show one's skills

요즘 갑자기 요리 프로그램이 많아졌어요.

There are more cooking shows now than before.

갑자기 = all of a sudden, suddenly
프로그램 = program, TV show
-아/어/여지다 = to become + adjective

유명한 요리사가 새 레스토랑을 오픈했어요.

A famous chef has opened a new restaurant.

새 = new

레스토랑 = restaurant

A Korean word for a "restaurant" is "식당," but when you use "레스토랑" instead of "식당," it usually refers to a fancy or upscale restaurant that sells western-style cuisine, including Italian or French. Even if a restuarant is very fancy and expensive, if it's a Korean, Japanese, or Chinese restaurant, normally the word "레스토랑" is not used.

오픈하다 = to open a shop; there's a new shop opened.

해물 요리는 집에서 만들기가 조금 번거로워요.

It's really a hassle to make seafood dishes at home.

해물 = seafood

요리를 만들다 = to cook

조금 = a little

번거롭다 = to be hassling; to be inconvenient

WEEK 3 DAY 5

깨끗하다
to be clean

ⓒⓘⓞ *Andrius Repsys*

깨끗한 물
clean water

물 = water

깨끗한 바다
clean sea

바다 = sea, ocean

깨끗한 환경
clean environment

환경 = environment

깨끗한 창문
clean window

창문 = window

깨끗한 나라
clean country

나라 = country

깨끗한 공기
clean air

공기 = air

깨끗한 피부
clean skin; clear skin

피부 = skin

깨끗한 화장실
clean bathroom; clean toilet

화장실 = toilet; bathroom

집이 아주 깨끗해졌어요.
The house has become really clean.

아주 = very, really

피부가 참 깨끗하신 것 같아요.
Your skin seems very clear.

- 것 같다 = It seems/looks like + S + V

여기는 길거리가 참 깨끗하네요.
The street here is very clean.

길거리 = street

제가 컵을 깨끗하게 씻어 올게요.
I'll go wash the cup clean.

컵 = cup
씻다 = to wash
-아/어/여 오다 = to go + V + and come back

정리정돈만 잘해도 깨끗해 보여요.
Just by tidying things up well, it (the place) looks clean.

정리정돈하다 = to tidy things up
-아/어/여 보이다 = to look + adjective

깨끗한 사무실에서 일하니까 좋아요.
It's good to work in a clean office.

사무실 = office
일하다 = to work

제가 유리창을 깨끗하게 닦아 놨어요.
I have wiped the windows clean.

유리창 = (glass) window
닦다 = to wipe

손을 깨끗하게 씻어야 감기에 안 걸려요.

You should wash your hands so that you won't catch a cold.

손 = hand
-아/어/여야 = should + V₁ + in order to + V₂
감기 = cold, flu
감기에 걸리다 = to catch a cold

유리창이 너무 깨끗해서 없는 줄 알았어요.
The window was really clean, so I thought it wasn't there.

-(으/느)ㄴ 줄 알다 = to mistakenly think + S + V

책상이 깨끗해야 일도 더 잘 되는 것 같아요.
I feel like I can work better when my desk is clean.

책상 = desk
더 = more
잘 되다 = to become successful; to become fine

깨끗한 공기를 마시니까 기분이 정말 좋아요.
Getting some fresh air makes me feel really good.

마시다 = to drink
기분 = feelings; mood
정말 = really; very

오늘 손님이 오니까 사무실을 깨끗하게 청소해요.
A guest is coming today, so let's clean up the office.

손님 = guest, visitor
오다 = to come
청소하다 = to clean up

냄새
smell, odor

Andrius Repsys

좋은 냄새
good smell

좋은 is the adjective form of 좋다.

독특한 냄새
unique smell

독특하다 = to be unique
독특한 is the adjective form of 독특하다.

이상한 냄새
weird smell

이상하다 = to be weird, odd, strange
이상한 is the adjective form of 이상하다.

냄새가 나다
something smells

냄새를 맡다
to smell (something)

맡다 = to smell

이거 무슨 냄새예요?
What is this smell?

무슨 = what; what kind of

뭔가 타는 냄새 안 나요?
Don't you smell something burning?

뭔가 = something (subject)
뭔가 is the contracted form of 무언가.
타다 = to burn; to get tan
냄새가 나다 = something smells

바다 냄새가 너무 좋아요.
I really like the smell of the sea.

이상한 냄새가 나지 않아요?
Don't you smell something strange?

이거 냄새 한번 맡아 보세요.
Try smelling this.

-아/어/여 보세요 = Please try + V-ing

맛있는 냄새가 나는 것 같아요.
I think I smell something delicious.

맛있다 = to be delicious
맛있는 is the adjective form of 맛있다.

이 종이에서는 꽃 냄새가 나요.
This paper smells like a flower.

종이 = paper
꽃 = flower

이 냄새는 어디에서 나는 거죠?
Where is the smell coming from?

이걸 넣으면 냄새가 좋아질 거예요.
If you put this in, it will make it smell better.

이걸 = this (object)
넣다 = to put (something) in
좋아지다 = to become good/fine
이걸 is the contracted form of 이거를.

맛있는 냄새가 나서 더 배고파졌어요.
Because of the delicious smell, I feel more hungry now.

배고프다 = to be hungry, to be starving

냄새가 나는 물건은 밖에 내놓으세요.
Put the stuff that smells outside.

물건 = thing, item, stuff, belonging
밖 = outside
내놓다 = to put something outside

어디에선가 좋은 냄새가 나는 것 같아요.

I think there's a good smell coming from somewhere.

어디에선가 = from somewhere

청소를 하고 나면 냄새가 없어질 거예요.

After cleaning, the smell will disappear.

청소 = cleaning
청소를 하다 = to clean
-고 나면 = once + S + finish + V-ing
없어지다 = to disappear

그 음식은 맛은 있는데 냄새가 이상해요.

That food is delicious, but it smells weird.

그 = the; that
음식 = food
맛이 있다 = to be delicious

그 옷은 냄새가 나니까 빨아야 할 것 같아요.
Those clothes smell, so I think you should wash them.

옷 = clothes, outfit
빨다 = to wash one's clothes
-아/어/여야 하다 = should; have to; must

지저분하다

to be messy; to be dirty

ⓒ①⊚ 선경화

지저분한 방
messy room

방 = room

지저분한 거리
dirty street

거리 = street

지저분하게 먹다
to eat in a messy way

책상이 지저분하다
desk is messy

별로 안 지저분한데요?
It is not that messy.

별로 = not particularly, not very, not so much, not really
별로 안 -(으)ㄴ데요? = I don't think + S + be + that + adjective

바닥이 너무 지저분해요.
The floors are too dirty.

바닥 = floor

윤아 씨 방은 너무 지저분해요.
Yoona's room is too messy.

여기 너무 지저분해서 있기 싫어요.
This place is so dirty, I do not want to be here.

싫다 = to be not likable, to not like; to be unpleasant; to not enjoy, to hate

방이 정말 지저분하네요. 좀 치우세요.
The room is really messy. Please tidy it up.

치우다 = to clean up, tidy up; to move

이렇게 지저분한 방에서 어떻게 살아요?

How can you live in a room this messy?

이렇게 = like this, in this manner; so +adjective
어떻게 = how
살다 = to live

옷이 너무 지저분해서 옷 좀 갈아입고 갈 게요.
I will come after I change my clothes since my clothes are too dirty.

갈아입다 = to change (clothes)

지저분하다

눈 오는 날 신었더니 제 부츠가 지저분해
졌어요.

My boots became dirty because I wore them on a snowy
day.

눈 = snow
눈(이) 오다 = to snow
날 = day
신다 = to wear (footwear/socks)
부츠 = boots

미용실에 오래 못 갔더니 머리가 너무 지
저분해요.

My hair is really messy because I was unable to go to the
hair salon for a long time.

미용실 = hair salon
오래 = for a long time, a long time
못 = can't
머리 = head; hair

다른 자리는 괜찮은데 왜 경은 씨 자리만
지저분해요?

Why is it that Kyeong-eun's desk is messy while others'
are clean?

다른 = other; another
자리 = space, spot, seat, position; occasion
괜찮다 = to be okay, to be alright; to be nice
-만 = only; just

방이 이렇게 지저분한데 어떻게 공부를
한다는 거예요?

How can you say that you can study when the room is
this messy?

공부를 하다 = to study
어떻게 -(느)ㄴ다는 거예요? = How can you say
that you can/are going to + V?

제 동생은 아직 어려서 밥을 먹을 때 지
저분하게 먹어요.

My brother is still young, so when he is eating his meals,
he is messy.
My brother is still young, so he's a messy eater.

동생 = younger sister/brother
어리다 = to be young

저기 선반 위가 너무 지저분한 것 같은데
같이 치울까요?

I think the top of the shelf is too dirty. Shall we clean it
together?

저기 = there
선반 = shelf
위 = above; on; up
같이 = together; with + N
-(으)ㄹ까요? = Shall we + S + V?; Do you want
me to + V?; Should we + V?; Let's + V.

서랍 속이 너무 지저분해서 안 쓰는 물건
은 모두 버렸어요.

Since the inside of my drawer was so messy,
I threw out all the things I don't use.

서랍 = drawer (of desk or dresser)
속 = inside
모두 = all; every; everyone
버리다 = to throw away; to dump

어린 사촌 동생들이 놀러 와서 방을 지저분하게 어질렀어요.

My younger cousins came over and dirtied up the room.
My younger cousins came over and made a mess in the room.

어린 is the adjective form of 어리다.
사촌 = cousin
놀러 오다 = to come over to hang out; to visit to hang out
-아/어/여서 = by + V-ing; to + V + and (then)
어지르다 = to make a mess

그저께 내린 눈이 녹기 시작하면서 도로가 지저분해졌어요.

As the snow that fell the day before yesterday started to melt, the streets became dirty.

그저께 = the day before yesterday
눈(이) 내리다 = to snow
녹다 = to melt
시작하다 = to start, begin
도로 = road

Week 4

Day 1   **Audio Track : 22**
기다리다 [gi-da-ri-da]
to wait

Day 2   **Audio Track : 23**
운동 [un-dong]
exercise, workout; sport(s)

Day 3   **Audio Track : 24**
뛰다 [ttwi-da]
to run; to jump

Day 4   **Audio Track : 25**
길 [gil]
road, street; way

Day 5   **Audio Track : 26**
걷다 [geot-tta]
to walk

Day 6   **Audio Track : 27**
요일 [yo-il]
day of the week

Day 7   **Audio Track : 28**
앉다 [an-tta]
to sit

기다리다
to wait

오래 기다리다
to wait for a long time

오래 = for a long time, a long time

안에서 기다리다
to wait inside

안 = in; inside

손꼽아 기다리다
to eagerly look forward to something; to count the days waiting for something

손꼽다 = to count something on one's fingers

한참을 기다리다
to wait for a long while

한참 = for a long while

차례를 기다리다
to wait for one's turn

차례 = one's turn

친구를 기다리다
to wait for one's friend

친구 = friend

끝까지 기다리다
to wait it out; to wait until the end

끝 = end, finish
-까지 = until; to

오래 기다렸어요?
Have you been waiting for long?

잠깐만 기다려 주세요.
Wait for a moment, please.

잠깐 = short time; for a moment
-만 = only; just
-아/어/여 주세요 = (polite) Please do + something + for me

친구를 기다리고 있어요.
I am waiting for my friend.

-고 있다 = to be + V-ing

더 이상 못 기다리겠어요.
I can't wait any longer.

더 이상 = (not) any longer
못 = can't

아무리 기다려도 답장이 없어요.
No matter how long I wait, there's no reply.

아무리 -아/어/여도 = no matter how + adjective + S + V
답장 = reply

없다 = to not have; to be not there; to not exist

기다리고 기다리던 날이 왔어요.

The day I've been waiting for has come.
The day has arrived.

기다리고 기다리던 = N + that + S + was eagerly looking forward to

친구들을 기다리면서 책을 읽었어요.

I read a book while I was waiting for my friends.

-들 is a suffix used to indicate plural.
-(으)면서 = while + S + V-ing
책 = book
읽다 = to read

내일은 손꼽아 기다리던 소풍날이에요.

Tomorrow is the picnic day that I have been eagerly awaiting.

내일 = tomorrow
소풍 = picnic
날 = day

한참을 기다려도 안 와서, 전화를 해 봤어요.

I'm calling you because I've waited for a long time and you are still not here.

-아/어/여도 = even though; no matter how much + S + V
안 = not
오다 = to come
-아/어/여서 = because, since
전화 = phone call; telephone
전화를 하다 = to make a phone call
-아/어/여 보다 = to try + V-ing

끝까지 기다려 보세요. 좋은 일이 있을 거예요.

Wait it out. Good things will happen.

-(으)세요 = (polite) imperative
좋다 = to be good, likable; to be desirable; to be nice; to like
좋은 is the adjective form of 좋다.
일 = work; task; thing, stuff; occasion
-(으)ㄹ 것이다 = will; to be going to + V

기다리지 말고 주무세요. 저 늦게 들어올 거예요.

Don't wait for me and please go to bed. I will come home late.

주무시다 = (honorific) to sleep
저 = (polite) I; me
늦다 = to be late
늦게 is the adverb form of 늦다.
들어오다 = to come in

추우니까 밖에서 기다리지 말고 안에서 기다려요.

Since it's cold outside, don't wait outside, wait inside instead.

춥다 = to be cold
-(으)니까 = since, because
밖 = outside

줄을 서서 제 차례를 기다리고 있었는데 누가 새치기를 했어요.

I was waiting in line for my turn, and someone cut in line.

줄 = line
서다 = to stand; to stop
줄을 서다 = to wait in line
제 = (polite) my; I
누가 = who; someone (subject)
새치기를 하다 = to cut in line

운동
exercise, workout;
sport(s)

ⓒ①ⓞ *Lilian Phu*

준비 운동
warm-up exercise

준비 = preparation

운동 부족
lack of exercise

부족 = lack, shortage

운동 선수
athlete

선수 = athlete, sports player

운동하다
to do exercise; to work out

하다 = to do

운동을 좋아하다
to like working out

좋아하다 = to like

운동 좋아하세요?
Do you like working out?

어떤 운동 좋아하세요?
What kind of exercise do you like?

어떤 = what kind of; which

공원에 가서 같이 운동해요.
Let's go to the park and work out together.

공원 = park
가다 = to go; to leave
같이 = together; with + N

운동하는 거 별로 안 좋아해요.
I don't like exercising that much.

별로 = not particularly, not very, not so much, not really

운동을 너무 많이 해서 피곤해요.
I did quite a lot of exercise, so I am tired.

많다 = to be a lot
많이 is an adverb form of 많다.
피곤하다 = to be tired, exhausted; to be tiring

저는 운동하면서 음악을 많이 들어요.
I listen to a lot of music while I work out.

음악 = music
듣다 = to hear; to listen

살을 빼려면 굶지 말고 운동을 하세요.
In order to lose weight, don't skip meals, but exercise (instead).

살 = fat; flesh
빼다 = to subtract; to take something out
살을 빼다 = to lose weight
-(으)려면 = in order to + V
굶다 = to skip a meal; to starve

매일 저녁 헬스장에 가서 운동을 해요.
I go to the fitness center every evening and work out.

매일 = every day
저녁 = evening; dinner
헬스장 = gym

아침에 운동을 했더니 기분이 상쾌해요.
I went swimming this morning and I feel very good.

아침 = morning; breakfast
-았/었/였더니 = since/because + I/we + V-ed
기분 = feelings; mood
상쾌하다 = to be refreshing

수영을 하기 전에는 준비 운동을 해야 돼요.
Before you swim, you need to warm up.

수영 = swimming
-기 전에 = before + S + V
-아/어/여야 되다 = to have to + V

요즘 살을 빼기 위해서 운동을 하고 있어요.
I am exercising these days in order to lose weight.

요즘 = these days, lately
-기 위해서 = in order to + V

저 사람이 제가 제일 좋아하는 운동 선수예요.
That person is my favorite athlete.

사람 = person, people
제일 = the best; the most

매일 이렇게 피곤한 건 운동이 부족해서인 것 같아요.
I think the reason I am so tired every day is because of my lack of exercise.

이렇게 = like this, in this manner; so +adjective
부족하다 = to be insufficient; to not have enough + N
- 것 같다 = It seems/looks like + S + V

의사 선생님이 건강해지려면 운동을 해야 한다고 했어요.
The doctor told me that I need to do some exercise in order to become healthy.

의사 = doctor
선생님 = teacher
의사 선생님 is a more polite way to address a doctor than 의사. When people address/call a doctor in person, people often call them 선생님 or 의사 선생님.
건강하다 = to be healthy

-아/어/여지다 = to become + adjective
-(으)면 = if + S + V; when/once + S + V
-아/어/여야 하다 = should; have to; must
-다고 하다 = indirect ending - used to refer to what someone said

운동을 하는 건 안 좋아하지만, 스포츠 경기를 보는 건 좋아해요.
I don't like exercising, but I do like watching sports matches.

스포츠 = sport(s)
경기 = sport game, match
보다 = to see; to look; to watch; to meet up; to read

뛰다
to run; to jump

ⓒ①◎ 진석진

뛰어가다
to run somewhere
to run to a destination

빨리 뛰다
to run fast

빠르다 = to be fast
빨리 is an adverb form of 빠르다.

높이 뛰다
to jump high

높다 = to be high, tall
높이 is an adverb form of 높다.

펄쩍 뛰다
to jump (in a vigorous way)

펄쩍 is an adverb that describes how someone jumps vigorously or outrageously denies something.

천천히 뛰다
to run slowly

천천히 = slowly

늦었는데 뛸까요?
We are late, shall we run?

-(으)ㄹ까요? = Shall we + S + V?; Do you want me to + V?; Should we + V?; Let's + V.

뛰어도 늦을 것 같아요.
I think I will be late even if I run.

-(으)ㄹ 것 같다 = I think + S + will/be going to; it seems like + S + will/be going to

복도에서 뛰면 안 돼요.
You must not run in the hallway.

복도 = hallway, corridor
-(으)면 안 되다 = shouldn't; must not

좀 더 빨리 뛸 수 있어요?
Can you run a little faster?

좀 = a little; please
더 = more
-(으)ㄹ 수 있다 = can, to be able to; there is a chance that + S + V

뛰어왔더니 숨이 너무 차요.
I'm out of breath because I ran here.

숨이 차다 = to be out of breath

제가 금방 뛰어갔다 올게요.
I will quickly run over there and come back.

금방 = soon, shortly; quickly

저는 뛰는 거 정말 싫어해요.
I really don't like to run.

정말 = really; very
싫어하다 = to dislike, hate

저는 아침마다 10km씩 뛰어요.
I run 10km every morning.

-마다 = every + N
-씩 is a particle used for the amount that is
divided or repeated.

우리 이제 뛰어야 될 것 같아요.
I think we should run now.

우리 = we; us
이제 = now

급하게 뛰어 오다가 넘어졌어요.
I fell down because I was running in such a hurry to get here.

급하다 = to be urgent, pressing; to be hasty
급하게 is an adverb form of 급하다.
-다가 = as a result of + V-ing
넘어지다 = to fall (down); to trip

어디를 그렇게 급하게 뛰어가요?
Where are you running off to in such a hurry?

어디 = where; somewhere
그렇게 = like that; such + adjective/adverb

뛰어가면 힘드니까 그냥 걸어가요.
It's exhausting to run, so let's just walk.

힘들다 = to be difficult, hard, tough; to have a
hard time; to be tiring; to be tired
그냥 = just, only, simply
걸어가다 = to go on foot; to walk to + place
-아/어/여요 = imperative ending; Let's + V

뛸 필요 없어요. 그냥 걸어가도 돼요.
There is no need to run. We can just walk.

-(으)ㄹ 필요 없다 = to not need to + V
-아/어/여도 되다 = to be okay to + V

여기에서 거기까지 뛰어가면 얼마나 걸려요?
How long does it take to run from here to there?

여기 = here, this place
거기 = there, that place
얼마나 = how + adjective/adverb
(시간이) 걸리다 = to take (a certain amount of
time)

약속 시간에 늦어서 버스에서 내리자마자 뛰어갔어요.
I had to run as soon as I got off the bus because I was late for my meeting.

약속 = plans; promise
시간 = time; hour
버스 = bus
내리다 = to get off (from a vehicle)
-자마자 = as soon as + S + V

길

road, street; way

길거리
street; ground

거리 = street

지름길
shortcut

오르막길
uphill road

오르막 = uphill, ascent

막다른 길
dead end

막다르다 = to be a dead end

길을 잃다
to lose one's way; to get lost

잃다 = to lose

길을 걷다
to walk the road

걷다 = to walk

길을 건너다
to cross the road

건너다 = to cross (a street)

길을 물어보다
to ask the way

물어보다 = to ask

길을 잃은 것 같아요.
I think I lost the way.
I think I am lost.

-(으/느)ㄴ 것 같다 = It seems/looks like + S + V;
I think + S + V

길 좀 여쭤봐도 될까요?
May I ask you how to get there?
Do you mind telling me the way to get there?

여쭤보다 = (honorific) to ask

이 길이 아닌 것 같아요.
I don't think this is the way.

이 = this
아니다 = to be not

이 길로 가면 더 빨라요.
If you go this way, it is faster.

제가 지름길을 알고 있어요.
I know a shortcut.

알다 = to know

여기에서 어느 길로 가야 하나요?
Which way should I go from here?

어느 = which; some

어떤 사람이 길을 막고 서 있어요.
Someone is blocking the road.
There is someone standing in the road, blocking it.

어떤 사람 = someone; which person
막다 = to block
서 있다 = to be standing

길을 물어보는 게 좋을 것 같아요.
I think it's better if we ask for directions.

나가는 길이 어디인지 알려 주세요.
Please tell me which way is the way out.

나가다 = to go out
알려 주다 = to let someone know; to teach
something to someone

**이 길이 아닌가 봐요. 여긴 막다른 길이
에요.**
This must not be the way. It is a dead end.

-(으)ㄴ가 보다 = I think/guess + S + be + N, N +
must be + adjective
여긴 is a contraction of 여기 + 는.

**어제 길을 걸어가다가 친구를 우연히 만
났어요.**
I met a friend by chance yesterday while walking down
the street.

어제 = yesterday
우연히 = by chance
만나다 = to meet (up)

**길을 건널 때는 차가 오나 안 오나 잘 보
고 건너야 돼요.**
When crossing the street, you must carefully look to see
if a car is coming or not, then proceed.

-(으)ㄹ 때 = when/while + S + V
차 = car
-나 안 -나 = if + S + V or not
잘 = well; carefully

걷다
to walk

걸어가다
to walk; to walk to a place; to walk away

_____

걸어오다
to walk toward (a place); to come on foot

_____

빨리 걷다
to walk fast

_____

길을 걷다
to walk on the street

길 = road, street; way

_____

천천히 걷다
to walk slowly

_____

쉬지 않고 걷다
to walk without taking a break

쉬다 = to take a break; to get some rest

_____

세 시간 걸었어요.
I walked for three hours.

셋 = three (native Korean number)
세 is the adjective form of 셋.

_____

같이 조금 걸을까요?
Shall we walk a little?

조금 = a little

_____

그냥 좀 걷고 싶어요.
I just want to walk a little.

-고 싶다 = to want to + V

_____

많이 걸어서 피곤해요.
I walked a lot so I'm tired.

_____

걸어서 갈 수 있는 거리예요?
Is it a walkable distance?

거리 = distance

어떻게 여기까지 걸어왔어요?
How did you walk all the way here?

어떻게 = how

저는 여기서부터 걸어가면 돼요.
I can walk from here.

-(으)면 되다 = to be just supposed to + V; to just have to + V; can just + V

적당히 걷는 것은 건강에 좋대요.
I heard that moderate walking is good for your health.

적당하다 = to be moderate
적당히 is an adverb form of 적당하다.
건강 = one's health
-대요 = I heard that + S + V; They say + S + V

택시를 못 잡아서 그냥 걸어왔어요.
I couldn't get a cab, so I just walked here.

택시 = cab, taxi
잡다 = to hold; to grab
택시를 잡다 = to get a cab

정말로 거기까지 걸어서 갈 거예요?
Are you really going to walk all the way there?

정말로 = really

어제 너무 많이 걸어서 다리가 아파요.
I walked so much yesterday that my legs hurt.

다리 = leg
아프다 = to be sick, hurt

계속 걸어가다 보면 왼쪽에 보일 거예요.

If you keep walking, you will see it on your left.

계속 = repeatedly, again and again, continuously
-다 보면 = if + S + keep + V-ing
왼쪽 = left (side)
보이다 = to be seen; to be able to see

너무 많이 걸으면 피곤하니까 조금만 걸으세요.
Walking too much will tire you out, so walk just a little.

저는 회사에서 가까운 곳에 살아서 걸어서 출근할 수 있어요.
I live near my office, so I can walk to work.

회사 = company; office
가깝다 = to be near, close
가까운 is the adjective form of 가깝다.
곳 = place
살다 = to live
출근하다 = to go to work

WEEK 4 DAY 6

요일
day of the week

ⓒ ⓕ ⓞ 마법사

무슨 요일에 만날까요?
Which day of the week shall we meet?

무슨 = what; what kind of

오늘이 무슨 요일이죠?
Which day of the week is it today?
What day is today?

오늘 = today

다음 주 토요일에 뭐 해요?
What are you doing next Saturday?

다음 = next
주 = week
토요일 = Saturday
*월요일 = Monday, 화요일 = Tuesday, 수요일 =
Wednesday, 목요일 = Thursday, 금요일 = Friday,
일요일 = Sunday
뭐 = what; something
뭐 is the contracted form of 무엇.

다른 요일날 가면 안 돼요?
Can't we go some other day of the week?

다른 = other, another
요일날 is the same as 요일 and is often used in
spoken language.
-(으)면 안 돼요? = Can/Can't I...?

저는 월요일이 정말 싫어요.
I really hate Mondays.

싫다 = to be not likable, to not like; to be
unpleasant; to not enjoy, to hate

무슨 요일을 제일 좋아해요?
Which day of the week do you like most?

다음 주 화요일까지는 바빠요.
I am busy until next Tuesday.

바쁘다 = to be busy

저는 주로 수요일에 한가해요.
I am usually free on Wednesdays.

주로 = usually
한가하다 = to be free (time-wise); to not have
many things to do

무슨 요일에 만나는 게 좋아요?
Which day of the week is good to meet?

올해는 제 생일이 일요일이에요.
This year, my birthday is on a Sunday.

올해 = this year
생일 = birthday

올해 추석이 무슨 요일인지 알아요?
Do you know which day of the week Chuseok is on this year?

추석 is one of two major holidays in Korea. It is similar to Thanksgiving in the United States as it celebrates the yearly harvest.

저는 요일마다 출근하는 시간이 달라요.
I go to work at a different time every day of the week.

다르다 = to be different

무슨 요일날 가서 무슨 요일날 돌아와요?
Which day of the week do you leave and which day do you come back?
Which day of the week are you going and which day are you coming back?

돌아오다 = to return, to come back

그 가게가 무슨 요일에 문 닫는지 알아요?
Do you know which day of the week that store closes?

그 = the; that
가게 = store, shop
문 = door
닫다 = to close

혹시 지난 화요일에 대학로에 있지 않았어요?
Were you, by any chance, in Daehangno last Tuesday?

혹시 = by any chance
지난 = last
대학로 = Daehangno
대학로 is an area in downtown Seoul that is famous for having many theaters.
있다 = to be there; to exist; to have

저는 일요일에는 밖에 나가지 않고 잠만 자요.
I don't go outside on Sundays and just sleep.

잠을 자다 = to sleep

거기는 금요일 밤만 되면 사람이 너무 많아져요.
That place gets too crowded on Friday nights.

밤 = night
되다 = to become

저는 이번 주에는 어떤 요일에 만나도 상관 없어요.

I don't mind what day of the week we meet this week.

이번 = this; this time
상관 없다 = to not matter

그 사람은 저랑 같은 요일, 같은 시간에 수업을 들어요.

He attends classes on the same day of the week at the same time that I do.

그 사람 = that person; he, she
같다 = to be the same
같은 is the adjective form of 같다.
수업을 듣다 = to attend a class, take a class

그 날은 제가 시간이 안 될 것 같은데, 다른 요일에 시간 되는 때 없어요?

I don't think I will be able to make time that day, but is there any other day this week when you have time?

그 날 = that day, the day
시간이 되다 = to be able to make it; to have time
때 = time

앉다

to sit

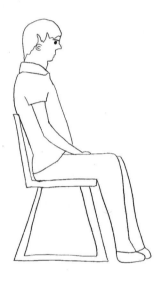

ⓒⓕⓞ 선경화

자리에 앉다
to sit down (on a seat)

자리 = space, spot, seat, position; occasion

여기 앉으세요.
Sit here.

똑바로 앉으세요.
Sit up straight.

똑바로 = straight (adverb)

앉으니까 편하죠?
It feels good to sit down, right?

편하다 = to be comfortable; to be convenient

앉을 데가 없어요.
There is no place to sit.

-(으)ㄹ 데 = place to + V

여기 앉아도 되나요?
Can I sit here?

이 소파에 앉아 보세요.
Now, sit on this sofa.

소파 = sofa

모두 자리에 앉아 주세요.
Everyone, please be seated.

모두 = all; every; everyone

다리 아파요. 앉고 싶어요.
My legs hurt. I want to sit down.

노약자석에는 앉으면 안 돼요.
You can't sit in the seats reserved for the elderly.

노약자석 = seats reserved for the elderly

우리 좀 앉아서 이야기할까요?
Shall we sit down for a second and talk?

우리 -(으)ㄹ까요? = Shall we ...?
이야기하다 = to talk, speak, say, tell; to have a conversation; to tell a story

앉다

저기 앉아 있는 사람은 누구예요?
Who is that person sitting there?

저기 = there
누구 = who

_____

여기 앉아 있던 사람 못 보셨어요?
Did you see the person who was sitting here?

_____

저 벤치에 앉아서 좀 쉬었다 가요.
Let's sit down on that bench there and rest before we walk again.

저 = that
벤치 = bench

저기요, 안 보이니까 좀 앉아 주세요.
Excuse me, I can't see (because of you), so please sit down.

저기요. = Excuse me.

_____

가만히 앉아 있으면 문제가 해결되지 않아요.
If you just sit there doing nothing, the problem won't be solved.

가만히 = still; motionlessly
문제 = problem; issue; thing; matter
해결되다 = to be solved

_____

지금 이 시간에 버스에 타면 앉을 자리가 있을까요?
If you take the bus at this hour, will there be any seats left?

지금 = now
지금 이 시간 = at this hour
타다 = to ride; to get on; to take (vehicle)

_____

어제 책상에 앉아서 공부하다가 잠이 들어 버렸어요.
I fell asleep yesterday while sitting in the chair and studying.

책상 = desk
공부하다 = to study
잠 = sleep
잠이 들다 = to fall asleep
-아/어/여 버리다 is used when talking about something that happened against your hope or expectations.

_____

가만히 앉아서 컴퓨터만 하지 말고 밖에 나가서 운동도 하세요.
Don't just sit there using your computer, but also go out and do some exercise.

컴퓨터 = computer
운동 = exercise; sports
-도 = too, also
운동하다 = to exercise, work out

Week 5

Day 1   Audio Track : 29

배우다 [bae-u-da]

to learn; to study

Day 2   Audio Track : 30

손 [son]

hand

Day 3   Audio Track : 31

잊다 [it-tta]

to forget

Day 4   Audio Track : 32

발 [bal]

foot

Day 5   Audio Track : 33

있다 [it-tta]

to be there; to exist; to have

Day 6   Audio Track : 34

눈 [nun]

eye

Day 7   Audio Track : 35

없다 [eop-tta]

to not have; to not be there; to not exist

배우다
to learn; to study

© ① ② 마법사

보고 배우다
to watch and learn; to learn by seeing others do something

보다 = to see; to look; to watch; to meet up; to read

술을 배우다
to learn to drink; to learn drinking manners

술 = alcohol

운전을 배우다
to learn to drive

운전 = driving

혼자서 배우다
to learn by oneself

혼자서 = alone, by oneself

한국어를 배우다
to learn Korean

한국어 = the Korean language

학교에서 배우다
to learn in school

학교 = school

한국어 어디에서 배웠어요?
Where did you learn Korean?

어디 = where; somewhere

아버지한테서 술을 배웠어요.
I learned my drinking manners from my father.

아버지 = father

그런 말은 어디에서 배웠어요?
Where did you learn such an expression?

그런 = (something) like that; such + noun
말 = language; what one says; expression; word; term

그 사람은 뭐든지 빨리 배워요.
He learns everything fast.

그 = the; that
사람 = person, people
뭐든지 = whatever it is, anything

빠르다 = to be fast
빨리 is the adverb form of 빠르다.

20살 때 처음 운전을 배웠어요.
I learned how to drive for the first time when I was 20 years old.

-살 = age, years old
때 = time
처음 = first; for the first time

분명히 배웠는데 기억이 안 나요.
I'm sure I learned about it (before), but I can't remember.

분명히 = for sure, certainly, without doubt
기억 = memory
안 = not
기억이 나다 = to remember

배우다

기타를 배워 보려고 생각 중이에요.
I am thinking of learning to play the guitar.

기타 = guitar
-아/어/여 보다 = to try + V-ing
생각 = thought; opinion; idea
-(으)려고 생각 중이다 = to be thinking of + V-ing

어릴 때 피아노하고 발레를 배웠어요.
When I was young, I learned piano and ballet.

어리다 = to be young
-(으)ㄹ 때 = when/while + S + V
피아노 = piano
발레 = ballet

어제 배운 것을 벌써 다 잊어 버렸어요.
I've already forgotten what I learned yesterday.

어제 = yesterday
벌써 = already
다 = all; every (thing)
잊어버리다 = to forget

배우고 싶은 것은 많은데 시간이 없어요.

There are a lot of things I want to learn, but I have no time.

-고 싶다 = to want to + V
많다 = to be a lot
시간 = time; hour
없다 = to not have; to be not there; to not exist

영어는 배우면 배울수록 더 어려워지는 것 같아요.
The more English I learn, the more difficult it seems to become.

영어 = the English language
-(으)면 -(으)ㄹ수록 = the more ... the more ...
더 = more
어렵다 = to be difficult
-아/어/여지다 = to become + adjective
- 것 같다 = It seems/looks like + S + V

아이들은 어른들이 하는 행동을 금방 보고 배워요.
Kids watch what grown-ups do and learn really quickly.

아이 = child, kid; baby
-들 is a suffix used to indicate plural.
어른 = adult, grown-up
하다 = to do
행동 = behavior
금방 = soon, shortly; quickly

영어를 배우고 싶어하는 사람들이 많아지고 있어요.
There is an increasing number of people who want to learn English.

-고 싶어하다 = someone wants to + V

고등학교 때 스페인어를 배웠는데, 지금은 하나도 기억이 안 나요.
I learned Spanish back in high school, but I don't remember anything now.

고등학교 = high school
스페인어 = the Spanish language
지금 = now
하나도 = not even one; not at all

손
hand

ⓒ⊕⊚ *Kanari Pictures*

왼손
left hand

왼쪽 = left (side)
왼 is the adjective form of 왼쪽.

오른손
right hand

오른쪽 = right (side)
오른 is the adjective form of 오른쪽.

손을 들다
to raise one's hand

들다 = to raise; to pick (something) up

손을 대다
to touch

대다 = to touch; to apply something to something

손을 잡다
to hold one's hand

잡다 = to hold; to grab

손 들어!
Raise your hands!

손이 아파요.
My hand hurts.

아프다 = to be sick, hurt

손 줘 보세요.
Give me your hand.

주다 = to give
-(으)세요 = (polite) imperative

손을 다쳤어요.
My hand was injured.

다치다 = to get hurt, injured

손 씻고 올게요.
I will go wash my hands.

씻다 = to wash
오다 = to come

손이 참 예쁘시네요.
You have very beautiful hands.

참 = very, quite
예쁘다 = to be pretty

저는 왼손잡이예요.
I am left-handed.

저 = (polite) I; me
왼손잡이 = left-handed

너는 손이 없어? 니가 해.
Don't you have hands? Do it yourself!

너 = (casual) you
니 is origianlly 너, but people often just use 니 in casual conversations.

손에 들고 있는 거 뭐예요?
What is that thing that you have in your hand?

뭐 = what; something
뭐 is the contracted form of 무엇.

뜨거우니까 손 조심하세요.
It's hot, so be careful.

뜨겁다 = to be hot
조심하다 = to be careful

직접 제 손으로 만들었어요.
I made it with my own hands.

직접 = directly; by oneself; with one's own hands
만들다 = to make

손으로 눈을 비비지 마세요.
Don't rub your eyes with your hands.

눈 = eye
비비다 = to rub
-지 마세요 = (polite) Don't + V

어제 처음으로 손을 잡았어요.
Yesterday, we held hands for the first time.

어제 = yesterday

더러운 손으로 만지지 마세요.
Don't touch it with dirty hands.
Don't touch that with your dirty hands.

더럽다 = to be dirty
더러운 is the adjective form of 더럽다.
만지다 = to touch

정답을 아시는 분은 손 들어 주세요.
If you know the correct answer, please raise your hand.

정답 = correct answer
아시다 = (honorific) to know
분 = (honorific) person

잊다
to forget

ⓒⓘⓞ 선경화

깜빡 잊다
to completely forget (for a short period of time)
to just forget; to slip one's mind

잊어버리다
to forget

약속을 잊어버리다
to forget an appointment

약속 = plans; promise

까맣게 잊어버리다
to completely forget

시간 가는 것을 잊다
to forget the time passing

시간(이) 가다 = time passes, time goes

저랑 한 약속 잊으셨어요?
Did you forget the promise you made me?

약속을 하다 = to promise, make a promise

그 일을 잊을 수가 없어요.
I cannot forget about that incident.

일 = work; task; thing, stuff; occasion
-(으)ㄹ 수가 없다 = to be not able to + V, can't

여권 챙기는 거 잊지 마세요.
Don't forget to take your passport.
Don't forget to pack your passport.

여권 = passport
챙기다 = to take care; to take; to pack

잊지 말고 우유 좀 사다 주세요.
Please do not forget to buy and bring me some milk.

우유 = milk
좀 = a little; please
사다 = to buy

사다 주다 = to buy
something for some-
one and bring it to
that person

이미 지난 일이니 잊어버리세요.
It's a past incident, so forget about it.

이미 = already
지나다 = to pass

그 때 한 약속 벌써 잊은 거예요?
Did you already forget the promise you made back then?

그때 = at that time; back then

그 일을 어떻게 잊을 수가 있겠어요.
How can I forget that incident?

어떻게 = how
-(으)ㄹ 수가 있다 = can, to be able to; there is a
good chance that + S + V

매일 아침 꽃에 물 주는 거 잊지 마세요.

Don't forget to water the flowers every morning.

매일 = every day
아침 = morning; breakfast
꽃 = flower
물 주다 = to water; to give water

어떻게 제 생일을 잊어버릴 수가 있어요?

How could you forget my birthday?

제 = (polite) my; I
생일 = birthday

전화 드리기로 하고 깜빡 잊었네요. 죄송해요.

I said I would give you a call and it slipped my mind. I'm sorry.

전화 = phone call; telephone
전화 드리다 = (polite) to give one a call, to call
-기로 하다 = to plan to + V; to decide to + V; to make a promise to + V
-네요 is a sentence ending that expresses realization of a fact or agreement to a statement.
죄송해요. = (polite) I'm sorry.

너무 바빠서 밥 먹는 것도 잊어버리고 있었어요.

I was so busy that I forgot to eat.

너무 = too much, excessively; very
바쁘다 = to be busy
-아/어/여서 = because, since
밥 = food; meal; cooked rice
먹다 = to eat; to drink
-도 = too, also

비밀번호를 잊어버려서 로그인을 못 하고 있어요.

I forgot my password, so I am unable to log-in.

비밀번호 = password
로그인 = log-in
로그인을 하다 = to log-in
못 = can't
-고 있다 = to be + V-ing

친구랑 만나기로 약속하고는 까맣게 잊어버렸어요.

I made a plan (to meet up) with my friend and I completely forgot.

친구 = friend
만나다 = to meet (up)
-기로 약속하다 = to promise to + V

오늘 아침에 중요한 회의가 있다는 걸 잊고 있었어요.

I forgot that there was an important meeting this morning.

오늘 = today
중요하다 = to be important
중요한 is the adjective form of 중요하다.
회의 = meeting
있다 = to be there; to exist; to have

친구랑 오랜만에 만나서 시간 가는 것도 잊고 놀았어요.

I hung out with my friend and we ended up losing track of time.

오랜만에 = first time in a long period of time
놀다 = to play; to hang out

발
foot

발판
foothold, scaffold, support for the feet

평발
flat feet

_____

발소리
footstep

소리 = sound

_____

발냄새
foot odor

냄새 = smell, odor

_____

발자국
footprint

자국 = trail; mark; stain

_____

발가락
toe

_____

발 마사지
foot massage

마사지 = massage

_____

발이 작다
to have small feet

작다 = to be small, little

_____

발이 아프다
to have sore feet, pain in the feet

_____

발이 못생겼다
to have ugly feet

못생기다 = to be ugly

_____

발을 혹사시키다
to overwork one's feet

혹사시키다 = to overtax/overwork + N

_____

이 신발, 발에 잘 맞아요?
Do these shoes fit your feet well?

신발 = shoes
잘 = well; carefully
맞다 = to fit

My Weekly Korean Vocabulary Book 1

발소리가 들린 것 같아요.
I think I heard footsteps.

발소리 = footstep
들리다 = to be heard, audible; to sound

오래 걸어서 발이 너무 아파요.
I walked for a long time, so my feet hurt.

오래 = for long, for a long time
걷다 = to walk

발 마사지를 받으니까 정말 개운해요.
Now that I got a foot massage, I feel so refreshed.

받다 = to receive
-(으)니까 = since, because
정말 = really; very
개운하다 = to feel refreshed

저는 하이힐을 신으면 발이 너무 아파요.

When I wear high heels, my feet hurt badly.

하이힐 = high heels
신다 = to wear (footwear/socks)
-(으)면 = if + S + V; when/once + S + V
발 = foot

추운 데에 오래 있어서 발이 너무 시려요.

I stayed in a cold place for a long time, so my feet are really cold.

춥다 = to be cold
추운 is the adverb form of 춥다.
-ㄴ 데 = (adjective) + place
시리다 = (a body part) feels cold

저는 발이 평발이어서 달리기를 잘 못해요.
I have flat feet, so I'm not good at running.

평발 = flat feet
달리기 = running
달리기를 하다 = to run
잘 못하다 = to be not good at + V-ing

새로 산 신발 때문에 발에 물집이 생겼어요.
I have a blister on my foot because of my new shoes.

새로 = newly; (do something) over
때문에 = because (of), since
물집 = blister
생기다 = to come into being; to be formed; to be created; to appear

---

저는 발이 너무 작아서, 맞는 사이즈를 찾기가 어려워요.
My feet are too small, so it's hard to find my size.

사이즈 = size
찾다 = to find; to look for

있다

to be there; to exist;
to have

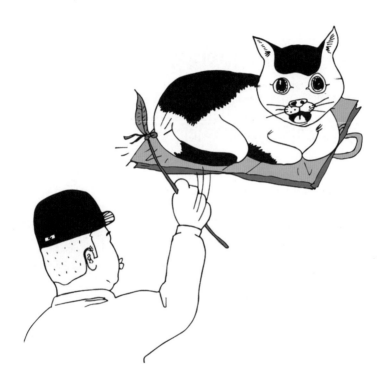

집에 있다
to be at home

집 = house, home

책이 있다
to have a book

책 = book

돈이 있다
to have money

돈 = money

가만히 있다
to stay still, not move

가만히 = still; motionlessly
가만히 있다 = to stay still, not move

수업이 있다
to have a class (to attend/teach)

수업 = class

약속이 있다
to have plans; to have someone to meet; to have somewhere to go

---

무슨 일 있어요?
Is there a problem?; Is there anything wrong?; What's going on?

무슨 = what; what kind of

여행 갈 돈 있어요?
Do you have money to go on a trip?

여행 = travel, trip
가다 = to go; to leave

어제 집에 있었어요?
Were you at home yesterday?

거실에 에어컨이 있어요.
There is an air conditioner in the living room.

거실 = living room
에어컨 = air conditioner

저기 아는 사람이 있어요.
There is someone I know.

저기 = there
알다 = to know

책상 위에 지우개가 있어요.
There is an eraser on the desk.

책상 = desk
위 = above; on; up
지우개 = an eraser

안에 누군가가 있는 것 같아요.
I think there is someone in there.
I think someone's in there.

안 = in; inside
누군가 = someone

우리 집에는 방이 세 개 있어요.
There are three rooms in my house.

우리 = we; us
집 = house, home
우리 집 = my house
방 = room

셋 = three (native Korean number)
세 is the adjective form of 셋.
개 is a general counter for inanimate objects.

움직이지 말고 가만히 좀 있어요.
Don't move and stay still.

움직이다 = to move

냉장고 안에 아이스크림이 있어요.
There is ice cream in the refrigerator.

냉장고 = refrigerator
아이스크림 = ice cream

잠깐만 여기 있어요. 금방 돌아올게요.
Stay here for a second. I will be right back.

잠깐 = short time; for a moment
-만 = only; just
여기 = here, this place
돌아오다 = to return; to come back
-(으)ㄹ 것이다 = will; to be going to + V

오늘은 약속이 있어서 먼저 가 볼게요.
I have to go somewhere today, so I'm going to leave first.

먼저 = first; before + N

저희 집은 여기에서 가까운 곳에 있어요.

My house is near here.

저희 = (polite) we; us; our
저희 집 = (polite) my house
가깝다 = to be near, close (in distance)
가까운 is the adjective form of 가깝다.

저는 3시에 수업이 있어서 지금 가 봐야 돼요.
I have a class at three, so I have to go now.

3시 = three o'clock
가 보다 = to leave (due to a previous engagement or time restriction)
-아/어/여야 되다 = to have to + V

eye

눈병
eye disease

병 = disease

큰 눈
big eyes

크다 = to be big; to be tall; to be loud
큰 is the adjective form of 크다.

눈을 뜨다
to open one's eyes

눈을 뜨다 = to open one's eyes; to wake up

눈을 감다
to close one's eyes

눈을 감다 = to close one's eyes

눈이 부시다
to be blinding, dazzling

눈이 부시다 = to be blinding, dazzling

눈병에 걸렸어요.
I've got an eye disease.

걸리다 = to be caught; to catch (a disease)
병에 걸리다 = to get sick

그 사람은 눈이 커요.
That person has big eyes.

눈에서 눈물이 났어요.
Tears started welling up in my eyes.

눈물 = tears
나다 = to come out
눈물이 나다 = tears flow; tears well up

그 여자는 눈이 예뻐요.
She has beautiful eyes.

여자 = girl, woman

눈을 크게 뜨고 보세요.
Open your eyes wide and look (at it closely).

크게 is an adverb form of 크다.

눈에 뭐가 들어간 것 같아요.
I think something got in my eye.

들어가다 = to go/come in

밤새 울었더니 눈이 부었어요.
I cried all night long, so my eyes are swollen.

밤새 = overnight; all night long
울다 = to cry
-더니 = S + V-ed + and as a result
붓다 = to swell

너무 졸려서 자꾸 눈이 감겨요.
I am so sleepy that my eyes keep closing.

졸리다 = to be sleepy
자꾸 = repeatedly, again and again
눈이 감기다 = eyes close

눈 감아 보세요. 선물이 있어요.
Close your eyes. I have a present for you.

선물 = gift, present

친구의 거짓말을 눈 감아 줬어요.
I turned a blind eye to my friend's lie.

거짓말 = lie
눈 감아 주다 = to turn a blind eye to something; to pretend not to have seen something happen

햇살이 너무 강해서 눈이 부셔요.
The sun is so bright that it's blinding.

햇살 = sunshine
강하다 = to be strong

오늘 아침에는 눈이 일찍 떠졌어요.
I woke up early this morning.

일찍 = early; soon
눈이 떠지다 = to wake up (without trying to)

눈이 따가울 때는 어떻게 해야 돼요?
When my eyes sting, what should I do?

따갑다 = to sting

아침에 눈을 뜨자마자 커피를 마셨어요.
As soon as I woke up this morning, I drank coffee.

-자마자 = as soon as + S + V
커피 = coffee
마시다 = to drink

눈이 잘 안 보여서 안경을 쓰기 시작했어요.
I couldn't see things clearly, so I started wearing glasses.

보이다 = to be seen; to be able to see
눈이 잘 안 보이다 = to be unable to see things well
안경 = glasses
쓰다 = to wear (eyewear, hat)
-기 시작하다 = to start + V-ing

없다

to not have; to not be there;
to not exist

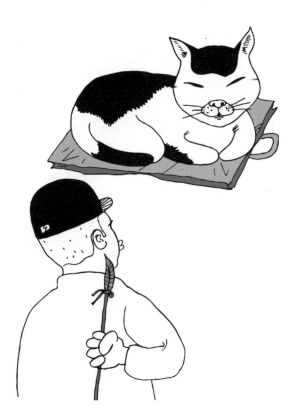

돈이 없다
to have no money

시간이 없다
to have no time

방법이 없다
there is no way; to have no solution

방법 = method, way

입맛이 없다
to have no appetite

입맛 = appetite

이상이 없다
there is no abnormality
everything is fine

이상 = abnormality, something wrong

할 말이 없다
to have nothing to say

할 말 = something to say

아는 사람이 없다
to not know anyone
there is no one who knows

저는 할 말 없어요.
I don't have anything to say.

이렇게 해도 문제 없어요?
There's no problem even if we do it like this?
Even if we do it like this, there's no problem?

이렇게 = like this, in this manner; so +adjective
-아/어/여도 = even though; no matter how
much + S + V
문제 = problem; issue; thing; matter

요즘 별로 재미있는 일이 없어요.
These days, there is nothing very interesting going on.

요즘 = these days, lately
별로 = not particularly, not very, not so much,
not really
재미있다 = to be fun; to be funny; to be
interesting

입맛이 없어서 점심을 안 먹었어요.
I had no appetite, so I didn't have lunch.

점심 = lunch

가게에 사람이 아무도 없는 것 같아요.
I think there is no one in the store.
I think nobody is in the store.

가게 = store, shop
아무도 = nobody; anybody (always used with a negative sentence structure)

그 사람은 성격이 나빠서 친구가 없어요.
He has a bad personality, so he doesn't have any friends.

성격 = personality, disposition
나쁘다 = to be bad

이 신발을 사고 싶은데 지금 돈이 없어요.
I want to buy these shoes, but I don't have any money (on me) now.

제가 없는 동안에 제 강아지 좀 돌봐 주세요.
While I'm not here, please look after my dog.

동안 = during; while; for + period of time
강아지 = puppy
돌보다 = to take care of, look after
-아/어/여 주세요 = (polite) Please do + something + for me

인사를 하고 싶었는데 기회가 없어서 못 했어요.
I wanted to say hi, but I couldn't because I didn't have the opportunity.

인사 = greeting
인사하다 = to greet, say "hello"
기회 = chance, opportunity

핸드폰을 잃어버렸는데 찾을 방법이 있을까요?
I've lost my cellphone. Do you think there is a way I can find it?

핸드폰 = mobile phone
잃어버리다 = to lose + N

요즘에 회사에서 바빠서 영화 볼 시간이 없었어요.
I've been busy at work lately, so I haven't had time to watch movies.

회사 = company; office
영화 = movie

카메라를 떨어뜨렸는데 다행히도 카메라에 아무 이상이 없었어요.
I dropped my camera, but fortunately there was nothing wrong with the camera.

카메라 = camera
떨어뜨리다 = to drop
다행히도 = fortunately
아무 = (not) any

어제 분명히 열쇠를 서랍 안에 넣어 두었는데 지금 찾아 보니까 없어요.
I am sure that I put the key in the drawer yesterday, but now I can't find it.

열쇠 = key
서랍 = drawer (of desk or dresser)
넣다 = to put (something) in
두다 = to leave (something) at a place

Week 6

울다
to cry

밤새 울다
to cry all night long

밤 = night
밤새 = overnight; all night long

기뻐서 울다
to cry out of joy

기쁘다 = to be joyful, glad
-아/어/여서 = because, since

큰 소리로 울다
to cry out loud

크다 = to be big; to be tall; to be loud
큰 is the adjective form of 크다.
소리 = sound
큰 소리 = loud noise, loud sound

울지 마세요.
Don't cry.

-지 마세요 = (polite) Don't + V

그만 울어요.
Stop crying.

그만 -아/어/여요. = Stop + V-ing.; Now, let's just + V.

왜 울고 있어요?
Why are you crying?

왜 = why; for what reason; how come
-고 있다 = to be + V-ing

울고 싶었지만 참았어요.
I wanted to cry, but I held back.

-고 싶다 = to want to + V
-지만 = but, however; though
참다 = to suppress, to hold back

그 여자는 울 때도 예뻐요.
She is pretty even when she cries.

그 = the; that
여자 = girl, woman
-(으)ㄹ 때 = when/while + S + V
-도 = too, also
예쁘다 = to be pretty

너무 슬퍼서 밤새 울었어요.
I was so sad that I cried all night long.

너무 = too much, excessively; very
슬프다 = to be sad

너무 울어서 눈이 부었어요.
I cried so much that my eyes got swollen.

눈 = eye
붓다 = to swell

그 사람은 잘 우는 편이에요.
He tends to cry easily.

사람 = person, people
잘 = well; carefully
-(으/느)ㄴ 편이다 = to tend to + V

아기가 울다 지쳐 잠이 들었어요.
The baby cried himself to sleep.

아기 = baby	잠 = sleep
-다 지치다 = to get tired from + V-ing; to get tired while + V-ing	잠이 들다 = to fall asleep

아기가 배고파서 우는 것 같아요.
It seems like the baby is crying because she's hungry.

배고프다 = to be hungry, starving
- 것 같다 = It seems/looks like + S + V

상을 받고 너무 기뻐서 울었어요.
I was so happy to receive the award that I cried.

상 = prize
받다 = to receive

울지 말고 자세히 설명해 보세요.
Stop crying and explain it to me in detail.

자세하다 = to be specific, detailed 자세히 is an adverb form of 자세하다.	설명하다 = to explain -아/어/여 보다 = to try + V-ing -(으)세요 = (polite) imperative

어린 아이가 넘어져서 울고 있어요.
A kid fell down and is crying.

어리다 = to be young 어린 is the adjective form of 어리다.	아이 = child, kid; baby 넘어지다 = to fall (down); to trip

실컷 울었더니 기분이 좀 나아졌어요.
I cried my eyes out, and now I feel better.

실컷 = as much as one wishes, to one's heart's content -더니 = S + V-ed + and as a result	기분 = feelings; mood 좀 = a little; please 나아지다 = to get better; to improve

어제 슬픈 영화를 보고 많이 울었어요.
Yesterday, I watched a sad movie and cried a lot.

어제 = yesterday 슬픈 is the adjective form of 슬프다. 영화 = movie	보다 = to see; to look; to watch; to meet up; to read 많다 = to be a lot 많이 is an adverb form of 많다.

울지만 말고 무슨 일이 있었는지 말을 해 봐요.
Don't cry, just tell me what happened.

무슨 = what; what kind of 일 = work; task; thing, stuff; occasion 일이 있다 = something happened, something came up	말 = language; what one says; expression; word; term 말을 하다 = to speak; to talk; to tell; to say

울기만 한다고 문제가 해결되는 건 아니잖아요.
Crying doesn't solve the problem.

-기만 하다 = just + V, to only + V
문제 = problem, issue; thing; matter
해결되다 = to be solved
-잖아(요) is a sentence ending used most commonly when correcting another person's remark or when refreshing someone's memory.

짜증

irritation, annoyance

ⓒⓘⓞ 진석진

짜증 나는 일
something irritating

짜증이 나다
to be irritated/irritating; to be annoyed/annoying

짜증을 내다
to show irritation; to act irritated

짜증을 부리다
to show irritation; to act irritated

짜증 나게 하다
to annoy; to make (someone) annoyed

-게 하다 = to make someone/something + V

왜 그렇게 짜증을 내요?
Why are you acting irritated like that?

그렇게 = like that; such + adjective/adverb

그 사람은 맨날 짜증 내요.
He always acts irritated.; He's always irritated.

그 사람 = that person; he, she
맨날 = every day; all the time

무슨 짜증 나는 일 있어요?
Is there something that's irritating (you)?
What's bugging you?

있다 = to be there; to exist; to have

짜증 내지 말고 즐겁게 해요.
Don't be annoyed, just be pleasant about it.

즐겁다 = to be pleasant, enjoyable
즐겁게 is an adverb form of 즐겁다.
하다 = to do

짜증이 가득 섞인 목소리였어요.
It was a voice filled with irritation.

가득 = full, in full capacity
섞이다 = to be mixed; to blend; to be blended
목소리 = voice

그 사람은 저를 너무 짜증 나게 해요.
He makes me so irritated.

저 = (polite) I; me

아기가 배가 고픈지 짜증을 부리네요.
The baby is showing irritation. She seems hungry.

배가 고프다 = to be hungry
-(으)ㄴ지 = maybe because
-네요 is a sentence ending that expresses realization of a fact or agreement to a statement.

엘리베이터가 층마다 서니까 짜증 나요.
The elevator is stopping at every floor and it's annoying.

엘리베이터 = elevator
층 = floor
-마다 = every + N
서다 = to stand; to stop
-(으)니까 = since, because

아침부터 왜 그렇게 짜증을 내고 그래요?
Why have you been acting so annoyed since this morning?

아침 = morning; breakfast

몸이 안 좋아서 그런지 자꾸 짜증이 나요.
I keep getting irritated, and I think it's because I don't feel well.

몸 = body
안 = not
좋다 = to be good, likable; to be desirable; to be nice; to like
자꾸 = repeatedly, again and again

동생이 자꾸 제 옷을 몰래 입어서 너무 짜증 나요.
My younger sister keeps secretly wearing my clothes and it's so annoying!

동생 = younger sister/brother
제 = (polite) my; I
옷 = clothes, outfit
입다 = to wear

너무 그렇게 자주 짜증 내면 옆에 있는 사람도 짜증 나요.
If you keep acting irritated like that, people around you will also get annoyed.

자주 = often, frequently
-(으)면 = if + S + V; when/once + S + V
옆 = next (to); on the side (of); around

집안일을 아무도 안 도와줘서 혼자 다 하려니까 짜증 나요.
It's annoying that no one is helping with the housework and I have to do all of it alone.

집안일 = housework
아무도 = nobody; anybody (always used with a negative sentence structure)
도와주다 = to help, give a hand
혼자 = alone, by oneself
다 = all; every (thing)
-(으)려니까 = as one is about to + V

숙제가 많아서 바쁜데 동생이 옆에서 자꾸 짜증 나게 해요.

I'm busy because I have a lot of homework, but my younger brother, who's sitting next to me, keeps bugging me.

숙제 = homework, assignment
바쁘다 = to be busy

안 그래도 늦었는데 뭘 안 가져와서 집에 다시 가야 되니까 짜증 나요.

I'm already late and I'm annoyed since I have to go back home because I didn't bring something.

안 그래도 = already; anyway
늦다 = to be late
뭘 = what (object)
뭘 is the contracted form of 무엇을.
가져오다 = to bring
집 = house, home
다시 = again
가다 = to go; to leave
-아/어/여야 되다 = to have to + V

웃다

to laugh, smile

© ① ◎ *Andrius Repsys*

웃는 얼굴
smiling face

얼굴 = face

웃지 마세요.
Don't laugh.

웃어서 미안해요.
I'm sorry for laughing.

미안하다 = to be sorry; to feel bad

웃으면 복이 와요.
A smile will bring luck.

복 = luck
오다 = to come

환하게 웃어 주세요.
Show me a big smile.

환하다 = to be bright
환하게 is an adverb form of 환하다.
-아/어/여 주세요 = (polite) Please do + something + for me

웃을 일이 아니에요.
It's not something you can laugh about.
It's no laughing matter.

웃을 일 = something to laugh about, laughable matter

웃게 해 줘서 고마워요.
Thanks for making me smile.

-아/어/여 주다 = to do something for someone
고맙다 = to be grateful

웃으면 건강에 좋아요.
Smiling is good for your health.

건강 = one's health
-에 좋다 = to be good for + N

요즘 웃을 일이 없어요.
Lately, there's nothing to laugh about.

요즘 = these days, lately
없다 = to not have; to not be there; to not exist

안 웃겠다고 약속하세요.
Promise me you won't laugh.

약속하다 = to promise, make a promise

웃는 얼굴이 보기 좋아요.
You look good with a smile on your face.

-기 좋다 = to be good for + V-ing
보기 좋다 = to look good to see

웃지만 말고 말을 하세요.
Stop laughing and start talking.

사람들이 저를 보고 웃었어요.
People laughed at me.

-들 is a suffix used to indicate plural.

너무 많이 웃어서 배가 아파요.
I laughed so hard that my stomach hurts.

배 = stomach, belly
아프다 = to be sick, hurt

제 이야기를 듣고 웃으면 안 돼요.
You shouldn't laugh at my story.

이야기 = story; what one says
듣다 = to hear; to listen
-(으)면 안 되다 = shouldn't; must not

저도 모르게 큰 소리로 웃었어요.
Without even meaning to, I laughed out loud.

모르게 = without knowing; without meaning
to + V

웃고 떠드는 사이에 밤이 되었어요.
While we were laughing and talking, it had already
become nighttime.

떠들다 = to chat; to make noise
사이 = while + S +V; between; among
되다 = to become

웃으면 웃을수록 기분이 좋아져요.
The more you laugh, the better you will feel.

-(으)면 -(으)ㄹ수록 = the more..., the more...
-아/어/여지다 = to become + adjective

많이 웃었더니 스트레스가 풀렸어요.
I laughed a lot, and it helped me to relieve some stress.

스트레스 = stress
스트레스가 풀리다 = stress is relieved

한번 웃기 시작하니까 멈출 수가 없었어
요.
Once I started laughing, I couldn't stop it.

한번 = once, one time
-기 시작하다 = to start + V-ing
멈추다 = to stop
-(으)ㄹ 수가 없다 = to be not able to + V, can't

WEEK 6 DAY 4

걱정
worry, concern

걱정거리
worries; concerns; something to worry about

-거리 is used after certain nouns or verbs to mean "something to + V."

괜한 걱정
needless worries; groundless concerns

괜한 = useless

지나친 걱정
excessive concern

지나치다 = to be excessive, too much
지나친 is the adjective form of 지나치다.

걱정 없다
to be unnecessary to worry; to have nothing to worry about

걱정스럽다
to be worried, worrisome

걱정을 하다
to worry

걱정이 되다
to be worried, concerned

걱정이 있다
to have a problem/something to worry about

걱정을 끼치다
to make someone worry

끼치다 = to cause; to have an influence (on)

걱정하지 마세요.
Don't worry.

무슨 걱정 있어요?
Is there something that worries you?

내일 시험이 걱정 돼요.
I am worried about tomorrow's test.

내일 = tomorrow
시험 = test, exam
걱정이 되다 = to be worried

괜한 걱정은 하지 마세요.
Don't be worried about something unnecessary.
Don't waste your time worrying about it.

걱정하다 = to worry

걱정해 주셔서 감사합니다.
Thank you for your concern.

감사하다 = to be grateful
-아/어/여 주셔서 감사합니다 = (polite) Thank you for + V-ing.

걱정을 끼쳐 드려서 죄송해요.
I'm sorry for making you worry.

-아/어/여 드리다 = (honorific) to do something for someone
죄송하다 = (polite) to be sorry; to feel bad
죄송해요. = (polite) I'm sorry.; I feel bad.

그렇게 걱정 되면 직접 하세요.
If you are really that worried, do it yourself.

직접 = directly; by oneself; with one's own hands

그런 걱정은 안 해도 될 것 같아요.
I don't think you need to worry about something like that.

그런 = (something) like that; such + noun
걱정을 하다 = to worry
-아/어/여도 되다 = to be okay to + V
-(으)ㄹ 것 같다 = I think + S + will/be going to; it seems like + S + will/be going to

---

왜 그런 걱정스러운 얼굴을 하고 있어요?
Why do you look so worried?

걱정스럽다 = to be worrisome
걱정스러운 is the adjective form of 걱정스럽다.
-(으)ㄴ 얼굴을 하다 = to wear a(n) + adjective + expression; have a(n) + adjective + face

부모님께 걱정거리를 안겨 드린 것 같아서 죄송해요.
I feel bad because I feel like I've given my parents something to worry about.
I feel bad because I feel like I've caused my parents to worry.

걱정거리 = worries; concerns; something to worry about
부모님 = parents
안기다 = to give; to cause

그 사람은 맨날 걱정만 하고 문제를 해결하려고 하지 않아요.
He always worries about things and never tries to solve the problem.

-만 = only; just
해결하다 = to solve, to settle (a problem)
-(으)려고 하다 = to try + V-ing

재미있다

to be fun; to be funny;
to be interesting

ⓒ①◉ *Krishna*

재미없다
to be not funny; to be uninteresting; to be boring

재미있는 책
interesting book

재미있는 사람
funny person; interesting person

재미있었어요?
Was it fun?

그 책 재미있어요?
Is that book interesting?

어제 재미있었어요.
Yesterday was fun.

뭐가 그렇게 재미있어요?
What is so funny?

제 이야기가 재미없어요?
Is my story not interesting?

재미없어요. 그만하세요.
It's not funny. Stop it.

지금 하는 일 재미있어요?
Do you enjoy what you do now?

재미있는 이야기를 들었어요.
I heard a funny story.

재미없다 = to be not funny; to be not interesting; to be boring

_____

책 = book

_____

_____

_____

_____

_____

뭐 = what; something
뭐 is the contracted form of 무엇.

_____

_____

그만하다 = to stop

_____

지금 = now

_____

재미없는 농담 좀 그만하세요.
Stop telling lame jokes.

농담 = prank, joke, trick

그 사람 진짜 재미있는 것 같아요.
I think he is really funny.

진짜 = really; very

재미없으면 그냥 안 보면 되잖아요.
If it's not interesting, you can just not watch it.

그냥 = just, only, simply
-(으)면 되다 = to be just supposed to + V; to just have to + V; can just + V

한국어 공부하는 거 정말 재미있어요.
Studying Korean is really fun.

한국어 = the Korean language
공부 = studies; one's learning
정말 = really; very

지난 주에 진짜 재미있는 일이 있었어요.

Last week, something really funny happened.

지난 = last
주 = week

너무 재미있어서 집에 오고 싶지 않았어요.
I was having so much fun that I didn't want to come home.

그 영화 보고 나서 재미있는지 말해 주세요.
After you see that movie, tell me if it is interesting.

-고 나서 = after + V-ing
-는지 = whether or not
말하다 = to talk; to say; to speak; to tell

영화가 너무 재미없어서 보다가 잠이 들어 버렸어요.
The movie was so boring that I fell asleep while I was watching it.

-다가 = while + S + be + V-ing

그 수업은 별로 추천하고 싶지 않아요.
진짜 재미없거든요.
I don't really want to recommend that class. It's really boring.

수업 = class
별로 = not particularly, not very, not so much, not really
추천하다 = to recommend

재미있다

문제

problem, issue; thing;
matter

ⓒ①◎ 안효진

시험 문제
exam questions

사회 문제
social problem

사회 = society

개인적인 문제
personal problem

개인적이다 = to be personal; to be private

문제를 풀다
to solve a problem

풀다 = to solve; to resolve

문제가 있다
a problem exists; there is a problem

중요한 문제
an important matter

중요하다 = to be important
중요한 is the adjective form of 중요하다.

어려운 문제
a difficult problem

어려운 is the adjective form of 어렵다.

문제가 복잡하다
the problem is complicated

복잡하다 = complicated

문제를 일으키다
to cause a problem

일으키다 = to cause

문제를 처리하다
to take care of a problem

처리하다 = to take care of + N

문제를 해결하다
to (re)solve a problem

문제가 생겼어요.

A problem has appeared.; We have a problem.

생기다 = to come into being; to be created; to appear; to be formed

이 문제는 너무 어려워요.

This question is too difficult.

이 = this
어렵다 = to be difficult

그 사람은 맨날 문제를 일으켜요.

That person always causes problems.

이건 중요한 문제니까 잘 들으세요.

This is an important matter, so listen carefully.

시험 문제가 너무 어려워서 다 못 풀었어요.

The questions on the exam were too difficult, so I couldn't solve all of them.
The exam was too difficult, so I couldn't finish it.

못 = can't

그건 개인적인 문제라 말씀드릴 수가 없네요.

That is a personal matter, so I cannot tell you.

개인적인 is the adjective form of 개인적이다.
말씀드리다 = (polite) to talk; to say; to speak; to tell

핸드폰에 문제가 있는 것 같아요. 자꾸 꺼져요.

I think there is a problem with my phone. It keeps turning off.

핸드폰 = mobile phone
꺼지다 = N + turns off

저는 수학 문제 푸는데 시간이 너무 오래 걸려요.

It takes too much time for me to solve math problems.

수학 = math
시간 = time; hour
오래 = for a long time, a long time
-는 데(에) 시간이 걸리다 = to take (a certain amount of) time in + V-ing

그 사람은 문제를 해결하려고 하지 않고 피하려고만 해요.

That person never tries to solve the problem and only tries to avoid it.

피하다 = to avoid

지루하다

to be boring; to be bored

지루한 책
boring book

지루한 영화
boring movie

지루한 수업
boring class

지루한 사람
boring person

지루해 보여요.
You look bored.

-아/어/여 보이다 = to look + adjective

지루하지 않았어요?
Were you not bored?
Was it okay (and not boring)?

제 이야기가 지루하세요?
Is my story boring you?

그 수업은 너무 지루해요.
That class is too boring.

오늘 하루는 정말 지루했어요.
Today has been very boring.

하루 = one day

오늘은 할 일이 없어서 지루해요.
I have nothing to do today, so I'm bored.

할 일 = (some)thing to do

지루한 회의를 세 시간이나 했어요.
We had a boring meeting for three long hours.

회의 = meeting	세 is the adjective
셋 = three (native	form of 셋.
Korean number)	-이나 = as many as +
	number; as much as +
	amount

이렇게 지루한 드라마는 처음 봐요.
I have never watched a drama that's THIS boring.

이렇게 = like this,	드라마 = TV drama,
in this manner; so	soap opera
+adjective	처음 = first; for the
	first time

요즘은 너무 바빠서 지루할 틈이 없어요.

I've been so busy recently that there is no time to be bored.

-(으)ㄹ 틈이 없다 = there is no time to + V

처음에는 지루한데 나중에 재미있어져요.

It's boring in the beginning, but it gets more interesting later.

나중 = later
재미있다 = to be fun; to be funny; to be interesting

영화가 너무 지루해서 보다가 잠들었어요.

The movie was so boring that I fell asleep while I was watching it.

잠들다 = to fall asleep

지루하면 잠깐 밖에 나가서 바람 좀 쐬고 와요.

If you are bored, go out and get some fresh air.

잠깐 = short time; for a moment
밖 = outside
나가다 = to go out
바람 = wind
바람을 쐬다 = to get some fresh air

그 일은 돈은 많이 주는데 지루하고 재미가 없어요.

That job pays you well, but it's boring and not fun.

돈 = money
주다 = to give
재미가 없다 = to be not fun; to be not funny; to be not interesting; to be boring

아무리 지루해도 수업 시간에는 잠을 자면 안 돼요.

No matter how boring it is, you shouldn't sleep during class.

아무리 -아/어/여도 = no matter how + adjective + S + V
자다 = to sleep
잠을 자다 = to sleep

이 영화 지루할 것 같았는데 생각보다는 재미있어요.

I thought this movie would be boring, but it was more interesting than I thought.

생각보다 = ~ than one thought

이 책, 재미있을 것 같아서 샀는데 읽어 보니까 지루해요.

I bought this book because it looked interesting, but I've read some of it, and I find it boring.

읽다 = to read
-아/어/여 보니까 = once + S + V-ed; it turns out that ...

Week 7

Day 1   **Audio Track : 43**

크다 [keu-da]

to be big; to be tall; to be loud

Day 2   **Audio Track : 44**

돈 [don]

money

Day 3   **Audio Track : 45**

작다 [jak-tta]

to be small, little

Day 4   **Audio Track : 46**

시간 [si-gan]

time; hour

Day 5   **Audio Track : 47**

좋아하다 [jo-a-ha-da]

to like

Day 6   **Audio Track : 48**

머리 [meo-ri]

head; hair

Day 7   **Audio Track : 49**

싫어하다 [si-reo-ha-da]

to dislike, hate

크다

to be big; to be tall;
to be loud

큰 돈
big money; a large amount of money

돈 = money

큰 신발
big shoes

신발 = shoes

키가 크다
to be tall

키 = height

덩치가 크다
(someone) is big

덩치 = one's body size

일교차가 크다
big difference in daily temperature

일교차 = daily temperature difference

가능성이 크다
there's a high possibility; there's a good chance

가능성 = possibility

크게 말하다
to speak loudly; to speak up

말하다 = to talk; to say; to speak; to tell

많이 커요?
Is it really big?

많다 = to be a lot
많이 is an adverb form of 많다.

얼마나 커요?
How big is it?

얼마나 = how + adjective/adverb

별로 안 커요.
It's not that big.

별로 = not particularly, not very, not so much, not really
안 = not

이건 너무 커요.
This is too big.

이거 = this thing; this
이건 is the contracted form of 이거는.
너무 = too much, excessively; very

크면 클수록 좋아요.
The bigger, the better.

-(으)면 -(으)ㄹ수록 = the more..., the more...
좋다 = to be good, likable; to be desirable; to be nice; to like

더 큰 가방이 필요할 것 같아요.
I think I need a bigger bag.

더 = more
가방 = bag
필요하다 = to need; to be necessary
-(으)ㄹ 것 같다 = I think + S + will/be going to; it seems like + S + will/be going to

저는 그렇게 큰 돈을 벌어 본 적이 없어요.
I've never made so much money.

저 = (polite) I; me
그렇게 = like that; such + adjective/adverb
돈을 벌다 = to make/earn money
-아/어/여 본 적이 없다 = to have not + p.p.

인터넷으로 봤을 때는 이렇게 클지 몰랐어요.
When I saw it on the Internet, I didn't know it was going to be this big.

인터넷 = the Internet
보다 = to see; to look; to watch; to meet up
-(으)ㄹ 때 = when/while + S + V
이렇게 = like this, in this manner; so +adjective
모르다 = to not know

요즘 일교차가 커서 감기에 걸리는 사람이 많아요.
Since there's such a big difference in the daily temperature these days, many people are catching colds.

요즘 = these days, lately
-아/어/여서 = because, since
감기 = cold, flu
감기에 걸리다 = to catch a cold
사람 = person, people

저도 직접 본 적이 없어서 얼마나 큰지 모르겠어요.
I didn't see it for myself, so I don't know how big it is.

-도 = too, also
직접 = directly; by oneself; with one's own hands
-(으)ㄴ 적이 없다 = to have never + p.p.

예전 사무실보다 새 사무실이 훨씬 크다고 들었어요.
I heard the new office is a lot bigger than the old one.

예전 = before; previous
사무실 = office
-보다 = than + N
새 = new
훨씬 = a lot/far/much (+ more + adjective/adverb)

이 파일은 용량이 커서 이메일로는 보내기 힘들 것 같아요.
This file is big in volume, so I think it's difficult to send via e-mail.
This file is huge, so I think it's difficult to send it via e-mail.

이 = this
파일 = file; folder
용량 = capacity; volume
이메일 = e-mail
-기 힘들다 = to be difficult/hard to + V

지금처럼 차가 계속 막히면 1시간내로 도착 못 할 가능성이 크죠.
If the traffic continues to be so backed up, there's a good chance that we won't be able to arrive within an hour.

지금 = now
-처럼 = like + N
차 = car
차가 막히다 = the traffic is bad; the road is jammed with traffic
-(으)면 = if + S + V; when/once + S + V
1시간 = one hour
-내 = within (+ time)
도착하다 = to arrive
못 = can't

WEEK 7 DAY 2

돈
money

cc🅯🅭 마법사

용돈 pocket money; allowance	용돈 = pocket money; allowance
잔돈 small change	잘다 = (size) to be fine; to be little
돈을 벌다 to earn money	벌다 = to earn
돈을 쓰다 to spend money	쓰다 = to use; to spend (+ money)
돈을 갚다 to pay back, return money	갚다 = to pay back
돈을 빌리다 to borrow money	빌리다 = to borrow; to rent
돈이 모자라다 to lack money; to be short on money	모자라다 = to lack; to be short of, insufficient
돈이 없어요. I don't have money.	없다 = to not have, not exist; to be not there
돈 좀 주세요. Give me some money.	좀 = a little; please 주다 = to give -(으)세요 = (polite) imperative
돈을 많이 벌고 싶어요. I want to make a lot of money.	-고 싶다 = to want to + V
돈이 많았으면 좋겠어요. I wish I had a lot of money.	-았/었/였으면 좋겠다 = I wish + S + V-ed
돈 좀 빌려줄 수 있어요? Can you lend me some money?	빌려주다 = to lend -(으)ㄹ 수 있다 = can, to be able to; there is a chance that + S + V

지갑에 돈이 별로 없어요.
I don't have much money in my wallet.

지갑 = wallet, purse

돈을 갚을 방법이 없어요.
There is no way I can pay you back.

방법 = method, way

옷을 사느라 돈을 다 썼어요.
I spent all my money buying clothes.

옷 = clothes, outfit
사다 = to buy
-느라 = for + V-ing, while + V-ing
다 = all; every (thing)

돈이 많다고 행복한 건 아니에요.
Just because you have a lot of money doesn't mean you are happy.

-다고 = just because; saying that + S + V
행복하다 = to be happy

이번 달에는 돈을 너무 많이 썼어요.
I've spent too much money this month.

이번 = this; this time
달 = month

세상에는 돈으로 살 수 없는 것들이 더 많아요.
There are many things in life that you can't buy with money.

세상 = world
-(으)ㄹ 수 없다 = to be unable to + V; can't

돈은 버는 것도 중요하지만 쓰는 것도 중요해요.
Making money is important, but spending money is also important.

중요하다 = to be important

저 신발을 사고 싶은데 돈이 모자라서 못 사겠어요.
I want to buy shoes, but I can't because I don't have enough money.

못 -겠다 = I don't think + S + can + V

작다
to be small, little

to be
small

CCKorea

작은 소리
small sound

소리 = sound

작은 도시
small city

도시 = city

작은 문제
small problem

문제 = problem, issue; thing; matter

작은 실수
small mistake

실수 = mistake

키가 작다
to be short (in height)

키 = height

옷이 작다
the clothes are small

목소리가 작다
the voice is small

목소리 = voice

이렇게 작은 옷이 맞아요?
You can fit into an outfit this small?

맞다 = to fit

키가 작은 게 콤플렉스예요.
My inferiority complex is that I am short.

콤플렉스 is something one feels self-conscious about. It usually includes a body part and/or appearance.

친구들이 저를 키 작다고 놀려요.
My friends tease me for being short.

친구 = friend
-들 is a suffix used to indicate plural.
놀리다 = to tease; to make fun of; to mock

저에게는 작은 소망이 하나 있어요.
I have a small wish.

소망 = hope, wish
하나 = one (native Korean number)
있다 = to be there; to exist; to have

이 치마는 저한테 너무 작은 것 같아요.
I think this skirt is too small for me.

치마 = skirt
- 것 같다 = It seems/looks like + S + V

저는 키가 작아서 항상 하이힐만 신어요.

I am short, so I always wear high heels.

항상 = always, all the time
하이힐 = high heels
-만 = only; just
신다 = to wear (footwear/socks)

그 사람은 키는 작은데 목소리는 정말 커요.

He's short (in height), but has a really big voice.

그 사람 = that person; he, she
정말 = really; very
크다 = to be big; to be tall; to be loud

차가 너무 작아서 사람이 많이 못 탈 것 같아요.

The car is too small, so I don't think many people can get in it.

타다 = to ride; to get on; to take (vehicle)

가방이 너무 작아서 물건을 많이 넣을 수가 없어요.

The bag is too small, so I can't put many things in it.

물건 = thing, stuff; item; belonging
넣다 = to put (something) in
-(으)ㄹ 수가 없다 = to be not able to + V, can't

그 사람은 목소리가 너무 작아서 말을 알아듣기 힘들어요.

His voice is too small, so it's hard to understand his words.
He speaks too softly, so it's hard to understand what he's saying.

말 = language; what one says; expression; word, term
알아듣다 = to understand what one says

이 컴퓨터는 화면이 너무 작아서 보고 있으면 눈이 아파요.

This computer has such a small screen that my eyes hurt when I look at it.

컴퓨터 = computer
화면 = screen
-고 있다 = to be + V-ing
눈 = eye
아프다 = to be sick, hurt

그렇게 작은 체구에 어디서 그런 힘이 나오는지 모르겠어요.

I don't know where such strength comes from within such a small body.

그렇게 = like that
체구 = build, frame, the size of one's body
어디서 = where
어디서 is originally 어디에서, but people often just use 어디서 for the ease of pronunciation.
그런 = (something) like that; such + noun
힘 = strength, power, energy
나오다 = to come out

이 신발은 너무 작아서 저한테 안 맞아요. 조금 더 큰 걸 보여주세요.

These shoes don't fit me because they are too small. Please show me something a bit bigger.

조금 = a little
큰 is the adjective form of 크다.
보여주다 = to show, display

시간

time; hour

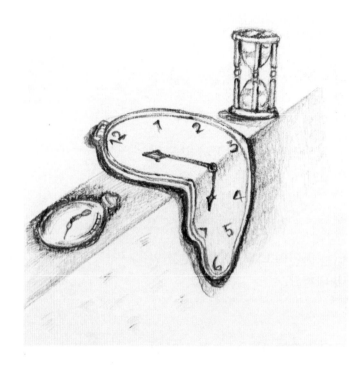

점심 시간
lunch time

점심 = lunch

시간 낭비
waste of time

낭비 = waste (of + N)

밥 먹는 시간
time to eat, time for eating

밥 = food; meal; cooked rice
먹다 = to eat; to drink

시간을 보내다
to spend time

시간을 아끼다
to save time

아끼다 = to save

시간을 물어보다
to ask the time

물어보다 = to ask

시간을 되돌리다
to turn back the time

되돌리다 = to turn back

시간 있어요?
Do you have time?

시간 다 됐어요.
Time's up.

시간이 다 되다 = time is up

시간 좀 내 주세요.
Please make some time for me.

시간을 내다 = to spare time; to make time
-아/어/여 주세요 = (polite) Please do + something + for me

수업 시간에 졸았어요.
I fell asleep in class.

수업 = class
졸다 = to doze off

시간 없다고 했잖아요.
I told you I don't have time.

-잖아(요) is a sentence ending used most commonly when correcting another person's remark or when refreshing someone's memory.

언제 시간 낼 수 있어요?
When can you make some time?

언제 = when

한 시간 정도 걸릴 것 같아요.
I think it will take about an hour.

한 시간 = one hour
정도 = about, around
(시간이) 걸리다 = to take (a certain amount of time)

점심 시간에 은행에 다녀올게요.
I will go to the bank during lunch time.

은행 = bank
다녀오다 = to go (to a place and come back)
-(으)ㄹ 것이다 = will; to be going to + V

서울에서 부산까지 몇 시간 걸려요?
How much time does it take to go from Seoul to Busan?

-까지 = until; to
몇 시간 = how many hours; a few hours

시간 가는 줄 모르고 수다를 떨었어요.
We chatted on without noticing the passage of time.

시간이 가다 = time passes
-는 줄 모르다 = to not know/notice + S + V
수다 = chatter
수다를 떨다 = to chatter

그 곳에 가는 건 시간 낭비라고 생각해요.
I think going there is a waste of time.

그 = the; that
곳 = place
가다 = to go; to leave
생각하다 = to think

지금 출발하면 거기까지 가는 데에 얼마나 걸릴까요?
If we leave now, how long do you think it will take to get there?

출발하다 = to depart
거기 = there, that place
-는 데(에) = in + V-ing, for + V-ing

시간을 되돌릴 수 있다면 초등학교 때로 돌아가고 싶어요.
If I could turn back the time, I'd want to go back to elementary school.

-(으)ㄹ 수 있다면 = if one could + V
초등학교 = elementary school
돌아가다 = to go back, return

좋아하다
to like

Michelle Smith

좋아하는 색
a color which one likes

좋아하는 사람
a person who one likes

좋아하는 드라마
a drama which one likes

제일 좋아하다
to like the most

커피 좋아하세요?
Do you like coffee?

아이들이 좋아할까요?
Will the children like it?

좋아하는 사람 있어요?
Is there anyone who you like?

어떤 영화 좋아하세요?
Which/What kind of movies do you like?

저는 혼자 있는 것을 좋아해요.
I like to be alone.

저는 등산을 별로 안 좋아해요.
I don't really like hiking.

이게 제가 제일 좋아하는 책이에요.
This is the book I like most.
This is my favorite book.

이 옷은 제가 제일 좋아하는 옷이에요.
This is the clothing I like the most.

색 = color

드라마 = TV drama, soap opera

제일 = the best; the most

커피 = coffee

아이 = child, kid; baby
-(으)ㄹ까요? = Shall we + S + V?; Do you want
me to + V?; Should we + V?; Let's + V.

어떤 = what kind of; which
영화 = movie

혼자 = alone, by oneself

등산 = mountain climbing, hiking

이게 = this (subject)
이게 is the contracted form of 이것이.
제 = (polite) my; I
제일 좋아하는 = one's favorite
책 = book

이렇게 하면 손님들이 좋아할 것 같아요.

If we do it like this, I think the customers will like it.

하다 = to do
손님 = guest; visitor

아이스크림 드실래요? 무슨 맛 좋아하세요?

Do you want to eat some ice cream? Which flavor do you like?

아이스크림 = ice cream
드시다 = (honorific) to eat; to drink
-(으)ㄹ래요? = Do you want to + V?; Shall we + V?
무슨 = what; what kind of
맛 = taste

외국어를 배우는 걸 좋아하는데 잘하지는 못 해요.

I like learning foreign languages, but I am not good at it.

외국어 = foreign language
배우다 = to learn; to study
잘하다 = to be good at something

제가 좋아하는 가수들이 다음 달에 콘서트를 할 거예요.

The singers that I like are going to have a concert next month.

가수 = singer
다음 = next
콘서트 = concert

스포츠를 하는 건 안 좋아하는데 보는 건 정말 좋아해요.

I don't like playing sports, but I really like watching them.

스포츠 = sport(s)
스포츠를 하다 = to play sports
보다 = to see; to look; to watch; to meet up

효진 씨가 좋아할 줄 알았는데 별로 안 좋아하는 것 같아요.

I thought Hyojin would like it, but I don't think she likes it very much.

-(으)ㄹ 줄 알다 = to know how to + V

제 친구들은 술 마시는 걸 좋아하는데 저는 별로 안 좋아해요.

My friends like to drink, but I don't really like it.

술 = alcohol
마시다 = to drink

저는 보통 학생들과 다르게 학창 시절 과목 중에 수학을 가장 좋아했었어요.

Unlike normal students, I liked math the most out of all the subjects when I was in school.

보통 = usually; normally; usual; normal; regular
학생 = student
다르다 = to be different
다르게 is an adverb form of 다르다.

학창 시절 = one's school days
과목 = subject (of study)
수학 = math
가장 = the most

머리

head; hair

ⓒⓘⓞ *Andrius Repsys*

긴 머리
long hair

길다 = to be long
긴 is the adjective form of 길다.

짧은 머리
short hair

짧다 = to be short
짧은 is the adjective form of 짧다.

머리를 감다
to wash one's hair

감다 = to wash (hair)

머리가 좋다
to be smart

머리를 빗다
to comb one's hair

빗다 = to comb

머리가 아프다
to have a headache

머리를 자르다
to get a haircut

자르다 = to cut

머리를 식히다
to clear one's head, rest one's mind

식히다 = to cool off

머리 조심하세요.
Watch your head.

조심하다 = to be careful

머리 기르고 싶어요.
I want to grow my hair long.

기르다 = to grow (one's hair/nails)

머리 염색하고 싶어요.
I want to dye my hair.

염색하다 = to dye

저는 아침에 머리를 감아요.
I wash my hair in the morning.

아침 = morning; breakfast

머리가 아파서 잠이 안 와요.
I have a headache, so I can't sleep.

-아/어/여서 = because, since
잠 = sleep
오다 = to come
잠이 오다 = to be sleepy; to feel drowsy
잠이 안 오다 = to be unable to sleep

머리가 아파서 약을 먹었어요.
I had a headache, so I took some pills.

약 = pill, medicine
약을 먹다 = to take pills/medicine

오늘은 머리가 잘 안 돌아가요.
My brain is slow today.

오늘 = today
잘 = well; carefully
머리가 안 돌아가다 = one's brain is slow, cannot think very quickly

머리를 자를까 생각 중이에요.
I'm thinking of getting a haircut.

-(으)ㄹ까 생각 중이다 = to be thinking of + V-ing

저는 머리가 긴 여자가 좋아요.
I like girls with long hair.

여자 = girl, woman

머리가 나쁘면 손발이 고생이에요.
If you are not smart, your body will pay for it.

나쁘다 = to be bad
머리가 나쁘다 = to be not smart; to be slow in understanding
손 = hand
발 = foot
고생 = hardship, trouble

그 사람은 정말 머리가 좋은 것 같아요.
I think he's really smart.

잠깐 밖에 나가서 머리 좀 식히고 올게요.
I will go out for a bit and get some fresh air.

잠깐 = short time; for a moment
밖 = outside
나가다 = to go out
식히다 = to cool off

싫어하다

to dislike, hate

싫어하는 일
things (to do) which you hate; job you hate

일 = work; task; thing, stuff; occasion

싫어하는 과목
a subject you hate

싫어하는 사람
a person you hate

벌레를 싫어하다
to hate bugs

벌레 = bug, insect

공부하기 싫어하다
to hate studying

공부하다 = to study

전 쇼핑하는 걸 싫어해요.
I hate shopping.

전 = (polite) I (subject)
전 is the contracted form of 저는.
쇼핑하다 = to do one's shopping, go shop

가끔은 싫어하는 일도 해야 돼요.
Sometimes you also have to do things you hate.

가끔 = sometimes
-아/어/여야 되다 = to have to + V

싫어하는 일이지만 꼭 해야 해요.
I hate (to do) this, but I have to do it.

-지만 = but, however; though
꼭 = for sure; at any cost; certainly; definitely;
make sure to (do something); tight
-아/어/여야 하다 = should; have to; must

그 사람이 저 싫어하는 거 같아요.
I think he hates me.

제 아들은 공부하기 너무 싫어해요.
My son really hates studying.

아들 = son
공부하다 = to study

그 사람은 지기 싫어하는 성격이에요.
He's the type (of person) who hates to lose.

지다 = to lose
성격 = personality, disposition

왜 자꾸 제가 싫어하는 행동을 하세요?
Why do you keep doing things I hate?

왜 = why; for what reason; how come
자꾸 = repeatedly, again and again
행동 = behavior

My Weekly Korean Vocabulary Book 1

싫어하는 건 아닌데 좋아하지도 않아요.
I don't hate it, but I don't like it either.

아니다 = to be not
좋아하다 = to like

저는 집안일 중에 설거지를 제일 싫어해요.
Among all the household chores, I hate washing dishes the most.

집안일 = housework
설거지 = dish washing

이 세상에 휴가를 싫어하는 사람은 없어요.
There is no one in this world who hates vacation.

휴가 = vacation, holiday

저는 우리 반에 싫어하는 사람이 한 명도 없어요.
There isn't anyone in the class I hate.

우리 = we; us
반 = class
명 = counter for people

제가 싫어하는 거 알면서 왜 자꾸 담배를 피워요?
You know I hate it, so why do you still keep smoking?

-(으)면서 = while + S + V-ing
왜 = why; for what reason; how come
자꾸 = repeatedly, again and again
담배를 피우다 = to smoke

저희 부모님은 제가 거짓말하는 걸 정말 싫어하세요.
My parents really hate me lying to them.
My parents really hate it when I lie.

저희 = (polite) we; us; our
부모님 = parents
거짓말하다 = to lie

저는 좋아하는 과목은 잘하는데 싫어하는 과목은 잘 못해요.
I'm good at the subjects I like, but I'm bad at the subjects I hate.

못하다 = to be bad at something, poor at something

높은 곳에서 갑자기 떨어지는 느낌을 싫어해서 놀이기구를 안 타요.
I really hate the feeling of suddenly dropping from a high place, so I don't go on amusement park rides.

높다 = to be high, tall
높은 is the adjective form of 높다.
떨어지다 = to fall, drop (down from somewhere), plummet
느낌 = feeling, sense
놀이기구 = amusement park rides
타다 = to ride; to get on; to take (vehicle)

Week 8

Day 1   **Audio Track : 50**
자다 [ja-da]
to sleep

Day 2   **Audio Track : 51**
잠 [jam]
sleep

Day 3   **Audio Track : 52**
일어나다 [i-reo-na-da]
to wake up; to get up

Day 4   **Audio Track : 53**
거짓말 [geo-jin-mal]
lie

Day 5   **Audio Track : 54**
만나다 [man-na-da]
to meet (up); to be seeing someone

Day 6   **Audio Track : 55**
사이 [sa-i]
relationship, relations

Day 7   **Audio Track : 56**
헤어지다 [he-eo-ji-da]
to part; to break up

자다
to sleep

늦게 자다
to go to bed late

늦다 = to be late
늦게 is the adverb form of 늦다.

일찍 자다
to go to bed early

일찍 = early; soon

낮잠을 자다
to take a nap

낮잠 = nap

늦잠을 자다
to wake up late

늦잠 = sleeping in, oversleeping

잘 잤어요?
Did you sleep well?

잘 = well; carefully

잠 안 자고 뭐 해요?
What are you still up doing?

잠 = sleep	뭐 is the contracted
안 = not	form of 무엇.
뭐 = what; something	하다 = to do

졸려요. 자고 싶어요.
I'm sleepy. I want to sleep.

졸리다 = to be sleepy
-고 싶다 = to want to + V

어제 몇 시에 잤어요?
What time did you go to bed yesterday?

어제 = yesterday
몇 시 = what time

피곤할 테니 일찍 자요.
You must be tired, so go to bed early.

피곤하다 = to be tired, exhausted; to be tiring
-(으)ㄹ 테니 = (assuming that) something must
+ V

잘 자고 내일 연락해요.
Good night and call me tomorrow.

내일 = tomorrow
연락하다 = to contact; to call, text

어제 한숨도 못 잤어요.
I couldn't sleep at all yesterday.

제 동생은 아직 자고 있어요.
My sister is still sleeping.

동생 = younger sister/brother
아직 = (not) yet
-고 있다 = to be + V-ing

내일은 친구 집에서 잘 거예요.
I'm going to sleep over at my friend's house tomorrow.

친구 = friend
집 = house, home

오늘 늦잠을 자서 학교에 지각했어요.
I got up late today, so I was late for school.

오늘 = today
늦잠을 자다 = to get up late, oversleep, sleep in
학교 = school
-에 지각하다 = to be late for + N

어젯밤에 자다가 이상한 꿈을 꾸었어요.
I had a strange dream while sleeping last night.

어젯밤 = last night
이상하다 = to be weird, odd, strange
꿈 = dream
꿈을 꾸다 = to have a dream; to dream

일요일에는 하루 종일 잠만 자고 싶어요.
On Sundays, I just want to sleep all day long.

일요일 = Sunday
하루 = one day
하루 종일 = all day long
-만 = only; just

너무 졸려서 점심 먹고 잠깐 낮잠을 잤어요.
I was so sleepy, so I took a short nap after having lunch.

너무 = too much, excessively; very
점심 = lunch
먹다 = to eat; to drink
잠깐 = short time; for a moment

어제 잠을 많이 못 자서 오늘 너무 피곤해요.
I couldn't sleep much yesterday, so I am very tired.

많다 = to be a lot
많이 is an adverb form of 많다.
못 = can't

요즘에 일이 많아서 잠을 많이 못 자고 있어요.
I have a lot of work to do these days, so I am not getting a lot of sleep.

요즘 = these days, lately
일 = work; task; thing, stuff; occasion

어젯밤에 자고 있는데 친구에게서 전화가 왔어요.
Last night when I was sleeping, I got a phone call from a friend.

전화가 오다 = to get a phone call

잠
sleep

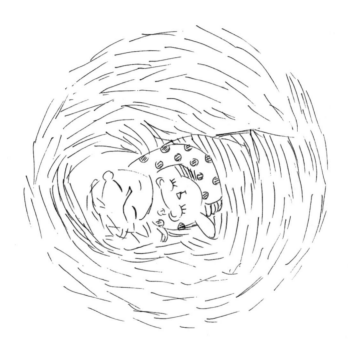

낮잠
nap

낮 = daytime

늦잠
sleeping late, getting up late

잠꼬대
talking in one's sleep

깊은 잠
deep sleep

깊다 = to be deep
깊은 is the adjective form of 깊다.

잠들다
to fall asleep

잠을 자다
to sleep

자다 = to sleep

잠이 많다
to sleep a lot

잠이 오다
to feel sleepy

오다 = to come

잠을 설치다
to not sleep very well

잠에서 깨다
to wake up from sleep

깨다 = to wake up

벌써 잠들면 안 돼요!
You can't fall asleep already!

벌써 = already
잠들다 = to fall asleep
-(으)면 안 되다 = shouldn't; must not

너무 더워서 잠이 안 와요.
It's too hot, so I can't sleep.

덥다 = to be hot
-아/어/여서 = because, since
잠이 오다 = to be sleepy; to feel drowsy
잠이 안 오다 = to be unable to sleep

오늘 아침에 늦잠을 잤어요.
This morning, I got up late.

아침 = morning; breakfast

그 사람은 잠꼬대가 심해요.
He talks a lot in his sleep.

그 사람 = that person; he, she
잠꼬대 = talking in one's sleep
심하다 = to be excessive, too much; to be harsh

저는 잠이 너무 많아서 문제예요.
I sleep too much and it's a problem.

저 = (polite) I; me
문제 = problem, issue; thing; matter

운전하다가 잠 오면 어떻게 해요?
What do you do when you feel sleepy while you are driving?

운전하다 = to drive
-다가 = as a result of V-ing
-(으)면 = if + S + V; when/once + S + V
어떻게 = how
-(으)면 어떻게 해요? = What do you do when + S + V ?; What am I supposed to do if you + V?

어제는 평소보다 잠을 늦게 잤어요.
I went to bed later than usual yesterday.

평소 = usual day, ordinary day
-보다 = than + N

어제 잠을 설쳐서 오늘 너무 피곤해요.
I didn't sleep well last night, so I feel very tired today.

잠을 설치다 = to not sleep very well

버스에서 잠들어서 내릴 곳을 놓쳤어요.
I fell asleep on the bus and missed my stop.

버스 = bus
내리다 = to get off (from a vehicle)
곳 = place
놓치다 = to miss

이렇게 시끄러운 데에서 어떻게 잠을 자요?
How do you sleep in such a noisy place?

이렇게 = like this, in this manner; so +adjective
시끄럽다 = to be noisy, loud
시끄러운 is the adjective form of 시끄럽다.
-ㄴ 데 = (adjective) + place

일어나다

to wake up; to get up

© ⓲ ⓳ *Dana Valle*

벌떡 일어나다
to stand up suddenly; to get up suddenly;
to spring up (out of one's seat)

벌떡 is an adverb that describes how someone
gets up or stands up suddenly and abruptly.

_____

일찍 일어나다
to wake up early

_____

먼저 일어나다
to leave early (before everyone else leaves)

먼저 = first; before + N

_____

아침에 일어나다
to wake up in the morning

_____

자리에서 일어나다
to get up from one's seat

자리 = space, spot, seat, position; occasion

_____

일어나세요.
Please wake up.; Please get up.; Please stand up.

-(으)세요 = (polite) imperative

_____

아직 안 일어났어요?
Are you awake yet?

_____

저는 먼저 일어날게요.
I'm leaving now (earlier than others).

-(으)ㄹ 것이다 = will; to be going to + V

_____

왜 이렇게 일찍 일어났어요?
Why did you wake up so early?

왜 = why; for what reason; how come

_____

방금 일어나서 아직도 졸려요.
I just woke up, so I am still sleepy.

방금 = just (now); a moment ago
아직도 = still, (not) yet

_____

오늘 아침에 몇 시에 일어났어요?
What time did you wake up this morning?

_____

오늘은 평소보다 일찍 일어났어요.
I woke up a bit earlier than usual today.

내일 일찍 일어나야 하니까 일찍 자요.

You have to wake up early tomorrow, so you should go to sleep early.

-아/어/여야 하다 = should; have to; must
-(으)니까 = since, because

저는 아침에 일어나는 게 정말 힘들어요.

It is really hard for me to wake up in the morning.

정말 = really; very
힘들다 = to be difficult, hard, tough; to have a hard time; to be tiring; to be tired

저는 아침에 일어나자마자 운동을 하러 가요.

I go exercise as soon as I wake up in the morning.

-자마자 = as soon as + S + V
운동 = exercise; sports
-(으)러 가다 = to go to + V

오늘 아침에는 일찍 일어나서 운동을 했어요.

This morning, I woke up early and exercised.

-아/어/여서 = by + V-ing; to + V-ing

공연이 끝나고 관객들이 모두 일어나서 박수를 쳤어요.

After the performance, the whole audience stood up and applauded.

공연 = performance, concert
끝나다 = to end; to be over
관객 = audience
-들 is a suffix used to indicate plural.
모두 = all; every; everyone
박수를 치다 = to applaud, clap

바닥 청소를 해야 하니까 모두 의자에서 일어나 주세요.

We have to clean the floor, so all (of you) please get up from your chairs.

바닥 = floor
청소 = cleaning
청소를 하다 = to clean
의자 = chair
-아/어/여 주세요 = (polite) Please do + something + for me

제가 지금 이름을 부르는 사람은 자리에서 일어나 주세요.

The people whose names I call now, please get up from your seats.

제 = (polite) my; I
지금 = now
이름 = name
이름을 부르다 = to call one's name

어제 술을 많이 마셨더니 아침에 일어나기가 정말 힘들었어요.

It was really hard to get up in the morning because I drank a lot yesterday.

술 = alcohol
마시다 = to drink
-았/었/였더니 = since/because + I/we + V-ed

거짓말
lie

ⓒ🅕🅓 마법사

거짓말쟁이
liar

뻔한 거짓말
obvious lie

뻔하다 = to be obvious
뻔한 is the adjective form of 뻔하다.

선의의 거짓말
white lie; lie with good intentions

선의 = good intentions

새빨간 거짓말
downright lie; lying through one's teeth

새빨갛다 = to be bright red, very red
새빨간 is the adjective form of 새빨갛다. When placed before the word 거짓말, it means "downright" or "total."

거짓말을 하다
to tell a lie

거짓말이죠?
You're lying, aren't you?

거짓말하지 마세요.
Please stop lying.

-지 마세요 = (polite) Don't + V

거짓말인 거 다 알아요.
I know it's all a lie.

다 = all; every (thing)
알다 = to know

제 말이 거짓말처럼 들려요?
Does it sound like I'm lying?

말 = language; what one says; expression; word, term
-처럼 = like + N
들리다 = to be heard, audible; to sound

그런 뻔한 거짓말에 누가 속아요?
Who would be deceived by such an obvious lie?

그런 = (something) like that; such + noun
누가 = who; someone (subject)
속다 = to be fooled, deceived

그런 뻔한 거짓말을 누가 믿어요?
Who believes such an obvious lie?

믿다 = to believe (in), trust

거짓말인지 정말인지 모르겠어요.
I don't know if it's a lie or the truth.

-인지 = whether
모르다 = to not know

거짓말하고 있는 것 같지 않아요?
Don't you think he's lying?

- 것 같다 = It seems/looks like + S + V
- 것 같지 않아요? = Don't you think + S + V ?

처음에는 저도 거짓말인 줄 알았어요.
I also thought that it was a lie at first.

처음 = first; for the first time
-도 = too, also
-인 줄 알다 = to mistakenly think + S + be + N

그 사람 거짓말쟁이니까 믿지 마세요.
He's a liar, so don't trust him.

그 = the; that
거짓말쟁이 = liar
-(이)니까 = since/because + S+ be + N

거짓말을 전혀 안 하는 사람은 없을 거예요.
I don't think there's anyone who doesn't lie at all.

전혀 = (not) at all
없다 = to not have, not exist; to be not there

어떻게 저한테 그런 거짓말을 할 수가 있어요?
How could you tell me such a lie?

어떻게 + -(으)ㄹ 수가 있어요? = How could you + V? How dare you + V?

그거 거짓말인 거 알고 있으니까 솔직하게 이야기해요.
I know that's a lie, so just tell me honestly.

그거 = that
솔직하다 = to be honest
솔직하게 is an adverb form of 솔직하다.
이야기하다 = to talk, speak, say, tell; to have a conversation; to tell a story

---

어렸을 때 거짓말을 많이 해서 엄마한테 자주 혼났어요.
When I was young, I would tell a lot of lies, so I was often scolded by my mom.

어리다 = to be young
-(으)ㄹ 때 = when/while + S + V
엄마 = mom
자주 = often, frequently
혼나다 = to get scolded

저도 거짓말을 하는 건 싫어하지만 이번에는 어쩔 수 없어요.
I hate to lie, but I can't help it this time.

싫어하다 = to dislike, hate
이번 = this; this time
어쩔 수 없다 = can't help, can't but; there is nothing + S + can do about

만나다

to meet (up); to be seeing someone

우연히 만나다
to run into someone

우연히 = by chance

_____

어떻게 만났어요?
How did you meet each other?

_____

우리 그만 만나요.
Let's stop seeing each other.

우리 = we; us
그만 -아/어/여요. = Stop + V-ing.; Now, let's just + V.

_____

만나서 얘기할까요?
Do you want to meet up and talk?

얘기하다 = 이야기하다 = to talk, speak, say, tell; to have a conversation; to tell a story

_____

우리 언제 만날까요?
When shall we meet?

언제 = when

_____

아직 만난 적 없어요.
I have not met him/her yet.

-(으)ㄴ 적 없다 = to have never p.p.

_____

직접 만난 적 있어요?
Have you ever met him/her in person?

직접 = in person, directly
-(으)ㄴ 적 있다 = to have + p.p.

_____

만나서 뭐 할 거예요?
What are you going to do when you meet him/her?

_____

만나자마자 싸웠어요.
We started to fight as soon as we met.

싸우다 = to fight

_____

어디에서 만나고 싶어요?
Where do you want to meet up?

어디 = where; somewhere

_____

만나지 말았어야 했어요.
I shouldn't have met him/her.

-지 말았어야 했다 = should have not + p.p.

너무 늦어서 못 만났어요.
It was too late, so we couldn't see each other.

요즘 만나는 사람 있어요?
Is there anyone you are seeing lately?

있다 = to be there; to exist; to have

친구들 못 만난 지 오래 됐어요.
It's been a long time since I have seen my friends.

-(으)ㄴ 지 오래 되다 = to have been a long time since

만날 시간을 정해서 알려 주세요.
Decide when to meet and let me know.

시간 = time; hour
정하다 = to decide
알려 주다 = to let someone know; to teach something to someone

우리는 만날 때마다 커피숍에 가요.
Whenever we meet up, we go to a coffee shop.

-(으)ㄹ 때마다 = whenever + S + V
커피숍 = coffee shop
가다 = to go; to leave

일단 만나 보면 생각이 바뀔 거예요.
Once you meet him/her, you will change your mind.

일단 = once (+ S + V); first of all
-아/어/여 보다 = to try V-ing
일단 -아/어/여 보면 = once + S + V₁, (S + will/ might + V₂)
생각 = thought; opinion; idea
바뀌다 = to change; to be changed

어제 길에서 친구를 우연히 만났어요.
Yesterday, I saw a friend on the street by chance.

길 = road, street; way

만나는 사람마다 저를 보고 웃었어요.
Everyone I met laughed at me.

-마다 = every + N
웃다 = to laugh, smile

만날 수만 있다면 뭐든지 할 거예요.
As long as I can meet him/her, I will do whatever it takes.

-(으)ㄹ 수만 있다면 = as long as + S + can + V
뭐든지 = whatever it is, anything

사이
relationship, relations

ⓒ🄯🄪 마법사

친구 사이
friend(ly) relation; friends

연인 사이
a couple

연인 = unmarried couple

친한 사이
close relation

친하다 = to be close (with other people)

사이가 좋다
to have a good relationship
to get along well

좋다 = to be good, likable; to be desirable; to be nice; to like

사이가 안 좋다
to have a bad relationship
to not get along well

어떻게 아는 사이예요?
How do you know each other?

두 사람 아는 사이였어요?
You two know each other?

둘 = two (native Korean number)
두 is the adjective form of 둘.

저희는 그냥 친구 사이예요.
We are just friends.

저희 = (polite) we; us; our
그냥 = just, only, simply

그 사람하고 어떤 사이예요?
What kind of relationship do you have with him/her?

어떤 = what kind of; which

우리 사이에 못 할 말이 어디 있어요?
What words are there that cannot be spoken between us?
Is there anything we can't tell each other?

말(을) 하다 = to say, speak, tell, talk

저는 부모님하고 사이가 아주 좋아요.
I have a good relationship with my parents.

부모님 = parents
아주 = very, really

여기에서 누구랑 사이가 제일 좋아요?

Who do you get along with the best with out of the people here?

여기 = here, this place
누구 = who
제일 = the best; the most

친구 사이에 부끄러울 게 뭐가 있어요?

What is there to be embarrased about between friends?

부끄럽다 = to be ashamed; to be shameful; to be embarrassed; to be embarrassing

그 사람하고 아는 사이인 줄 몰랐어요.

I didn't know you were acquainted with her.

-인 줄 모르다 = to not know/notice + S + be + N

룸메이트하고 사이 좋게 잘 지내고 있어요.

I am getting along well with my rommate.
I have a good report with my roommate.
I have a good relationship with my roommate.

룸메이트 = roommate
사이 좋게 지내다 = to get along

그 사람은 친구들 사이에서 인기가 많아요.

He is popular among his friends.

인기가 많다 = to be popular

저는 제 여동생하고 사이가 별로 안 좋아요.

I don't have a very good relationship with my younger sister.
I don't get along well with my younger sister.

여동생 = younger sister
별로 = not particularly, not very, not so much, not really

그 두 사람은 사이가 별로 안 좋은 것 같아요.

It seemed like the two people did not have a very good relationship.

그 두 사람이 그렇게 사이가 좋은 줄 몰랐어요.

I didn't know those two were in such a good relationship.

그렇게 = like that; such + adjective/adverb
-는 줄 모르다 = to not know/notice + S + V

지난번에 그 사람하고 싸워서 사이가 안 좋아졌어요.

I argued with him last time, and the relationship became bad.
I argued with him last time, and the relationship took a turn for the worst.

지난번 = last time

My Weekly Korean Vocabulary Book 1

헤어지다
to part; to break up

ⓒⓘⓞ 송미진

헤어지기 아쉽다
to feel sorry about parting ways

아쉽다 = to feel sorry (that something hap-
pened/did not happen/is happening/is not
happening)

_____

친구들과 헤어지다
to say goodbye to friends
to part ways with friends

여자친구와 헤어지다
to break up with one´s girlfriend

여자친구 = girlfriend

왜 헤어졌어요?
Why did you break up?

_____

우리 헤어졌어요.
We broke up.

_____

어떻게 헤어졌어요?
How did you break up?
How did you say goodbye?

_____

두 사람이 헤어졌는지 몰랐어요.
I did not know those two broke up.

_____

헤어진 여자친구가 자꾸 연락을 해요.
The girlfriend I broke up with keeps contacting me.

자꾸 = repeatedly, again and again
연락 = contact
연락을 하다 = to contact; to call, text

_____

**생각보다 일찍 헤어져서 집에 일찍 왔어
요.**
We parted earlier than I thought, so I came home early.

생각보다 = ~ than one thought

_____

**제가 알기로는 그 사람 남편하고 헤어졌
대요.**
As far as I know, that person parted ways with her
husband.

제가 알기로는 = as far as I know
남편 = husband
-대요 = I heard that + S + V; They say + S + V

_____

**어제 친구들과 놀다가 너무 늦게 헤어졌
어요.**
Since I hung out with my friends yesterday, we said
goodbye quite late.

놀다 = to play; to hang out

여자친구하고 왜 헤어졌는지 물어봐도 돼요?

Can I ask why you broke up with your girlfriend?

물어보다 = to ask
-아/어/여도 돼요? = Is it okay to + V?, Can + S + V?

그 사람은 아내와 헤어지고 지금은 혼자 산대요.

That person parted with his wife, and I heard he lives alone now.

아내 = wife
혼자 = alone, by oneself
살다 = to live

어제 친구들과 놀다가 헤어진 뒤에 서점 에 갔어요.

After saying goodbye to my friends while hanging out, I went to the bookstore.

-(으)ㄴ 뒤 = after + V-ing
서점 = bookstore

오랜만에 만났는데 이렇게 헤어지기 아 쉽지 않아요?

This is the first time we've met in a long time, don't you feel sad to part like this?

오랜만에 = first time in a long period of time
만나다 = to meet (up)

어제 친구랑 싸우고 헤어져서 너무 기분 이 안 좋아요.

Yesterday, I parted ways with a friend after we fought, so I really don't feel good.

기분 = feelings; mood

어제 강남에서 헤어진 뒤로 석진 씨하고 연락이 안 돼요.

After I parted with Seokjin yesterday in Gangnam, I haven't been able to reach him.

-(으)ㄴ 뒤로 = after + V-ing, ever since + S + V-ed
연락이 안 되다 = can't reach + person, can't contact

오랜만에 친구들을 만났는데 다들 바빠 서 금방 헤어졌어요.

I met my friends for the first time in a long time, but we parted ways soon after since everyone was busy.

바쁘다 = to be busy
금방 = soon, shortly; quickly

어제 길을 가다가 우연히 5년 전에 헤어 진 남자친구를 만났어요.

I ran into my ex-boyfriend, who I broke up with 5 years ago, while walking on the streets.

5년 = 5 years
전 = before, ago
남자친구 = boyfriend

영수 씨는 대학교 때 4년간 사귄 여자친구하고 졸업하자마자 헤어졌대요.

I heard Young Soo broke up with the girlfriend that he dated for 4 years as soon as he graduated.

대학교 = university
때 = time
4년 = four years
(amount of time) + -간 = for, during
졸업하다 = to graduate

Week 9

무섭다

to be scary; to be scared

무서운 꿈
scary dream

꿈 = dream

무서운 영화
scary movie

영화 = movie

무서운 이야기
scary story

이야기 = story; what one says

무서운 꿈을 꾸다
to have a scary dream

꿈을 꾸다 = to have a dream; to dream

무서운 이야기를 하다
to tell a scary story

이야기를 하다 = to talk, speak, say, tell; to have a conversation; to tell a story

안 무서워요?
Aren't you scared?
Isn't it scary?

안 = not

하나도 안 무서워요.
It's not scary at all.
I'm not scared at all.

하나도 = not even one; not at all

무서워하지 마세요.
Don't be afraid.

무서워하다 = to be afraid; to fear
-지 마세요 = (polite) Don't + V

안 무서운 척 하지 말아요.
Don't pretend you are not scared.

- 척 하다 = to pretend
-지 말아요. = Don't + V.

어제 본 영화 정말 무서웠어요.
The movie I saw yesterday was really scary.

어제 = yesterday
보다 = to see; to look; to watch; to meet up; to read
정말 = really; very

집에 혼자 있으면 정말 무서워요.
When I'm at home alone, it's really scary.

집 = house, home
혼자 = alone, by oneself
있다 = to be there; to exist; to have
-(으)면 = if + S + V; when/once + S + V

무서운 영화 보는 거 좋아하세요?
Do you like watching scary movies?

좋아하다 = to like

저는 무서운 놀이기구는 잘 못 타요.
I can't ride scary theme park rides very well.

저 = (polite) I; me	못 = can't
놀이기구 = amuse- ment park rides	타다 = to ride; to get on; to take (vehicle)
잘 = well; carefully	

이 영화 별로 안 무서우니까 걱정하지 마세요.
This movie is not that scary, so don't worry.

이 = this
별로 = not particularly, not very, not so much,
not really
-(으)니까 = since, because
걱정하다 = to worry

어제 무서운 영화를 봐서 밤에 무서운 꿈을 꿨어요.
I watched a scary movie yesterday, so I had a scary dream at night.

밤 = night

속으로는 무서웠지만 겉으로는 안 무서운 척 했어요.
I was scared on the inside, but I pretended that I wasn't scared.

속 = inside
-지만 = but, however; though
겉 = outside, exterior

옆집에 큰 개가 있는데 지나갈 때마다 너무 무서워요.
There is a huge dog next door that scares me every time I pass by it.

옆 = next
크다 = to be big; to be tall; to be loud
큰 is the adjective form of 크다.
개 = dog
지나가다 = to pass by, go past
-(으)ㄹ 때마다 = whenever + S + V
너무 = too much, excessively; very

친구한테 무서운 이야기를 들어서 밤에 잠을 못 잤어요.
I heard a scary story from my friend, so I couldn't sleep at night.

듣다 = to hear; to listen
잠 = sleep
잠을 자다 = to sleep

그 선생님은 평소에는 온화하신데 화가 나면 정말 무서우세요.
The teacher is usually mild-tempered, but when he gets mad, he's really scary.

그 = the; that
선생님 = teacher
평소 = usual day, ordinary day
온화하다 = to be mild-tempered; to be gentle,
mild-mannered
화 = anger
화가 나다 = to get angry/upset

어제 택시를 탔는데 기사 아저씨가 너무 빨리 운전해서 무서웠어요.

I took a taxi yesterday, but the driver drove too fast, so I was scared.

택시 = cab, taxi
기사 아저씨 = male driver (mainly of a bus or a taxi)
빠르다 = to be fast
빨리 is an adverb form of 빠르다.
운전하다 = to drive
-아/어/여서 = because, since

돕다

to help

cc🅯🅭 *Lilian Phu*

일을 돕다
to help someone in his/her work

일 = work; task; thing, stuff; occasion

서로 돕다
to help each other

서로 = each other

도와주다
to give someone a hand

도와주세요.
Please help me.

서로 도와야죠.
We need to help each other.

-아/어/여야죠 = You should + V; We need to + V

제가 도와 드릴까요?
Can I give you a hand?

제 = (polite) my; I
-아/어/여 드리다 = (honorific) to do something for someone
-(으)ㄹ까요? = Shall we + S + V?; Do you want me to + V?; Should we + V?; Let's + V.

언제 도와줄 수 있어요?
When can you help me?

언제 = when
-(으)ㄹ 수 있다 = can, to be able to; there is a chance that + S + V

도와주셔서 감사합니다.
Thank you for helping me.

-(으)셔서 = (honorific) because, since
감사합니다 = Thank you

이것 좀 도와줄 수 있어요?
Can you help me with this?

이것 = this; this thing
좀 = a little; please
-(으)ㄹ 수 있어요? = Can you + V?; Could you + V?

제가 어떻게 도와 드릴까요?
How can I help you?

어떻게 = how

도울 수 있을 때 많이 도와 드릴게요.
Let me help you out a lot while I can.

-(으)ㄹ 때 = when/while + S + V
많다 = to be a lot
많이 is an adverb form of 많다.
-(으)ㄹ 것이다 = will; to be going to + V

제가 도울 일 있으면 이야기해 주세요.

If there is something I can help you with, please let me know.

제가 도울 수 있는 일이 아닌 것 같아요.

I don't think that's something I can help you with.
I don't think I can help with this.

아니다 = to be not
-(으/느)ㄴ 것 같다 = It seems/looks like + S + V;
I think + S + V

친구가 숙제를 도와주기로 약속했어요.
My friend promised to help me with my homework.

친구 = friend
숙제 = homework
-기로 약속하다 = to promise to + V

친구가 이사하는 것 도와주러 갈 거예요.

I'm going to go to help my friend move.

이사하다 = to move in/out
-(으)러 가다 = to go to + V

제가 돕겠다고 했는데 그 사람이 거절했어요.

I offered to help, but he refused.

-다고 하다 = indirect ending - used to refer to
what someone said
그 사람 = that person; he, she
거절하다 = to reject, refuse, turn down

친구가 도와줘서 일이 생각보다 빨리 끝났어요.

Thanks to my friend's help, things have finished earlier than I expected.

생각보다 = ~ than one thought
끝나다 = to end; to be over

지금까지 도와준 사람들에게 선물을 주고 싶어요.

I want to give presents to the people who have helped (me) so far.

지금 = now	-들 is a suffix used to
-까지 = until; to	indicate plural.
사람 = person, people	주다 = to give
선물 = gift, present	-고 싶다 = to want
	to + V

저도 돕고 싶은데 지금 시간이 없어서 가봐야 할 것 같아요.

I also want to help you, but I don't have time now, so I think I should get going.

시간 = time; hour
없다 = to not have, not exist; to be not there
가 봐야 하다 = have to leave
-(으)ㄹ 것 같다 = I think + S + will/be going to;
it seems like + S + will/be going to

힘든 일이 있으면 언제든지 이야기하세요. 제가 도와 드릴게요.

If you have a challenging task, tell me at any time. I'll help you.

힘들다 = to be difficult, hard, tough; to have a
hard time; to be tiring; to be tired
힘든 is the adjective form of 힘들다.
언제든지 = whenever
-(으)세요 = (polite) imperative

이상하다

to be weird, odd,
strange

ⓒⓘⓞ *Andrius Repsys*

이상한 사람
strange person

맛이 이상하다
to taste weird

맛 = taste

날씨가 이상하다
the weather is strange

날씨 = weather

분위기가 이상하다
the atmosphere is strange

분위기 = atmosphere; ambience

얼굴색이 이상해요.
You look pale.

얼굴색 = how healthy one looks
얼굴색이 이상하다 = to look pale

이상하게 보지 마세요.
Don't judge me.

요즘 날씨가 이상해요.
The weather has been strange lately.

요즘 = these days, lately

뭔가 이상하지 않아요?
Don't you think something's strange?

뭔가 = something (subject)
뭔가 is the contracted form of 무언가.

진짜 이상한 성격이에요.
He has a really weird personality.

진짜 = really; very
성격 = personality, disposition

이상한 얘기 그만하세요.
Stop talking about such strange things.

얘기 = story; what one says
얘기 is the contracted form of 이야기.
그만하다 = to stop, to quit

오늘은 이상하게 피곤해요.
I feel strangely tired today.

오늘 = today
이상하게 is the adverb form of 이상하다.
피곤하다 = to be tired, exhausted; to be tiring

이상한 사람이 절 따라와요.
A weird person is following me.

절 = (polite) me
절 is the contracted form of 저를.
따라오다 = to follow (me)

몸이 이상해서 병원에 갔어요.
I didn't feel good, so I went to see a doctor.

몸 = body
병원 = hospital
가다 = to go; to leave

이 드라마는 결말이 이상해요.
This drama has a strange ending.

드라마 = TV drama, soap opera
결말 = a story's ending

자꾸 이상한 농담하지 마세요.
Stop pulling such weird pranks.

자꾸 = repeatedly, again and again
농담 = prank, joke, trick

어제 정말 이상한 꿈을 꿨어요.
I had a really weird dream last night.

조리법대로 했는데 맛이 이상해요.
I followed the recipe, but it tastes weird.

조리법 = recipe
-대로 = according to; as suggested by
하다 = to do

오늘따라 사무실 분위기가 이상해요.

Today, in particular, the atmosphere in the office is weird.

오늘따라 = today especially, today in particular
사무실 = office

이상해요. 어제 분명히 여기 놨는데 없어요.

It's strange. I put it here, for sure, but it's not here.

분명히 = for sure, certainly, without doubt
여기 = here, this place
놓다 = to place, put; to let go

커피 맛이 이상해서 봤더니 설탕 대신 소금을 넣은 거예요.
I wondered why the coffee tasted weird, and it turns out I had put in salt instead of sugar.

커피 = coffee
-았/었/였더니 = since/because + I/we + V-ed
설탕 = sugar
- 대신 = instead of + N/V-ing
소금 = salt
넣다 = to put (something) in

묻다

to ask

ⓒⓘⓞ 송미진

물어보다
to ask

길을 묻다
to ask for directions; to ask the way (to get somewhere)

길 = road, street; way

이유를 묻다
to ask the reason

이유 = reason

의견을 묻다
to ask one's opinion

의견 = opinion

친구에게 묻다
to ask a friend

뭐 좀 물어볼게요.
Let me ask you something.

뭐 = what; something
뭐 is the contracted form of 무엇.

언제든지 물어보세요.
Ask me anytime.

묻는 말에만 대답하세요.
Answer to only what you are asked.

말 = language; what one says; expression; word, term
-만 = only; just
대답하다 = to answer

가격이 얼마인지 물어봐 줄래요?
Can you ask how much the price is?

가격 = price
얼마 = how much
-(으)ㄹ래요? = Do you want to + V?; Shall we + V?

지금 제 의견을 물으시는 건가요?
Are you asking my opinion now?

제 = (polite) my; I

그만 좀 물어보세요. 저도 몰라요.
Please stop asking. I don't know either.

그만 -(으)세요. = Stop + V-ing.; Quit + V-ing
-도 = too, also
모르다 = to not know

모르는 게 있으면 저한테 물어보세요.
If you have something you don't know about, ask me.

길을 잃어서 지나가는 사람한테 물어봤어요.

I lost my way, so I asked a person passing by.

잃다 = to lose

제가 묻지도 않았는데 그 사람이 말해 줬어요.

I didn't even ask, but he told me (anyway).

-지도 않다 = to not even + V
말하다 = to talk; to say; to speak; to tell

저도 잘 모르는데 친구한테 한 번 물어볼게요.

I don't know (about that very) well, but I will ask my friend.

한 번 = once, one time

공부하다가 모르는 게 있으면 바로 물어보세요.

If you come across something you don't know while studying, ask (about it) right away.

공부하다 = to study
-다가 = as a result of V-ing
바로 = right away; straight; exactly; close(ly); right

저한테 묻지 말고 그 사람한테 직접 물어보세요.

Don't ask me, but ask him directly.

직접 = directly; by oneself; with one's own hands

물어보는 것이 자존심 상해요. 그냥 제가 알아볼게요.

If I ask, it'll hurt my pride. I'll just look into it myself.

자존심 = self-esteem, one's pride
상하다 = to hurt; to go bad
그냥 = just, only, simply
알아보다 = to investigate; to check up on; to find out; to search; to look into

제가 물어봤는데 그 사람이 제대로 대답을 안 해 줬어요.

I asked, but he didn't give me a proper answer.

제대로 = properly
대답을 하다 = to answer
안 = not

어제 물어볼 게 있어서 전화했는데 전화를 안 받으시더라고요.

I called you yesterday because I had something to ask, but you didn't answer the phone.

전화하다 = to call, make a phone call
전화 = phone call; telephone
전화를 받다 = to receive a phone call, pick up/answer the phone

화내다

to be angry at someone
to yell at someone out of anger

Andrius Repsys

화낼 일
something to be upset about

화내지 마세요.
Don't get angry.; Don't be upset.

저 화낸 적 없어요.
I wasn't angry.

-(으)ㄴ 적 없다 = to have never + p.p. (In this context, -(으)ㄴ 적 없다 means "No, I didn't.")

화내고 싶지 않아요.
I don't want to get angry.

-고 싶지 않다 = to not want to + V

저라도 화낼 것 같아요.
I think I would be angry, too.

-라도 = even

그건 화낼 일이 아니에요.
That's nothing to get upset about.

그건 = that (subject)
그건 is the contracted form of 그것은.
화낼 일 = something to be upset about

그 사람은 쉽게 화를 내요.
He gets angry easily.
He loses his temper easily.

쉽다 = to be easy
쉽게 is an adverb form of 쉽다.

계속 그러면 저도 화낼 거예요.
If you keep acting like that, I will get mad.

계속 = repeatedly, again and again, continuously
그러다 = to act like that, to behave like that

그만 화내고 이제 기분 풀어요.
Stop being upset (about it) and lighten up a bit.

그만 -고 = stop + V-ing and
이제 = now
기분 풀다 = to relieve anger in a mental (not physical) way; to calm down; to lighten up

부탁 안 들어 주면 화낼 거예요?
If I refuse your request, will you get angry (at me)?

부탁 = favor
부탁을 들어주다 = to grant one's favor

화낸다고 해결될 일이 아니에요.
Getting mad about it won't help solve the problem (for you).
Nothing changes, even if you get mad (at me).

-다고 = just because; saying that S + V
해결되다 = to be solved

그 사람이 화내는 거 처음 봤어요.
I've never seen him get angry before.

처음 = first; for the first time

그게 그렇게 심하게 화낼 일이에요?
Is that something that you need to get so upset about?

그게 = that, that thing (subject)
그게 is the contracted form of 그것이.
그렇게 = like that; such + adjective/adverb
심하다 = to be excessive, too much; to be harsh
심하게 is an adverb form of 심하다.

집에 늦게 가면 엄마가 화낼 거예요.
If I go home late, my mom will get mad.

늦다 = to be late
늦게 is the adverb form of 늦다.
엄마 = mom

제가 뭘 잘못 했길래 그렇게 화내요?
What have I done (to you) to make you get angry at me?

뭘 = what (object)
뭘 is the contracted form of 무엇을.
잘못하다 = to do something wrong; to do something bad to someone
-길래 = for what reason, resulting from which situation

그 사람은 사소한 일에도 맨날 화내요.
He always gets mad, even over small things.

사소하다 = to be trivial, minor, petty
사소한 is the adjective form of 사소하다.
맨날 = everyday; all the time

화내지 말고 제 이야기를 들어 보세요.
Don't get angry, but try listening to me.

-아/어/여 보다 = to try + V-ing

약속에 늦어서 친구가 저한테 화냈어요.
I was late, so my friend got mad at me.

약속 = plans; promise

저희 아버지는 화내실 때 정말 무서워요.

When my father gets angry, he is really scary.

저희 = (polite) we; us; our
아버지 = father
무섭다 = to be scary; to be scared

무조건 화내지 말고, 어떻게 할지 생각해 봐요.
Don't get mad without thinking, let's just think about how we can figure this out.

무조건 = no matter what, unconditionally, without considering other factors
-아/어/여요 = imperative; Let's + V

WEEK 9 DAY 6

생각
thought; opinion; idea

ⓒⓕⓞ 송미진

좋은 생각
good idea

좋다 = to be good, likable; to be desirable; to be nice; to like
좋은 is the adjective form of 좋다.

생각나다
to remember; to come to mind

다시 생각하다
to think again

다시 = again

신중히 생각하다
to think cautiously

신중하다 = to be cautious
신중히 is an adverb form of 신중하다.

가볍게 생각하다
to think lightly

가볍다 = to be light
가볍게 is an adverb form of 가볍다.

곰곰이 생각하다
to think carefully

곰곰이 = (to think) carefully

생각을 정리하다
organize one's thoughts

정리하다 = to organize; to tidy things up

잘 생각해 보세요.
Think carefully.

한번 생각해 볼게요.
I will think about it.

한번 -아/어/여 보다 = to try + V-ing

생각하면 할수록 화가 나요.
The more I think about it, the more upset I get.

-(으)면 -(으)ㄹ수록 = the more..., the more...

이렇게 생각해 본 적은 없어요.
I have never thought like this before.

이렇게 = like this, in this manner; so +adjective

답이 생각나는 사람은 손 드세요.
Anyone who remembers the correct answer, please raise your hand.

답 = answer; correct answer; reply
손 = hand
들다 = to raise; to pick (something) up

다시 생각해 봤는데, 저는 안 갈래요.
On second thought, I'm not going to go.

-(으)ㄹ래요. = I will ~, I will~; I'm going to ~.

중요한 일이니까 신중히 생각하세요.
Since it's an important matter, you should think (about it) carefully.

중요하다 = to be important
중요한 is the adjective form of 중요하다.
-(이)니까 = since/because + S+ be + N

그 이야기에 대해서 생각해 보셨어요?
Have you given it some thought?

-에 대해서 = about; regarding + N; concerning + N

아무리 생각해도 그건 틀린 것 같아요.
No matter how much I think about it, I still think it's wrong.

아무리 -아/어/여도 = no matter how + adjective + S + V
틀리다 = to be wrong

지금 드는 생각을 솔직하게 말해 보세요.

Please tell me honestly what comes to your mind.

들다 = to enter; to be categorized as; to be in
솔직하다 = to be honest
솔직하게 is the adverb form of 솔직하다.

열쇠를 어디에 두었는지 생각이 안 나요.

I don't remember where I put my key.

열쇠 = key
어디 = where; somewhere
두다 = to leave (something) at a place

곰곰이 생각해 봤는데, 이게 좋을 것 같아요.
I have given it a lot of thought and I think this will be good.

이게 = this (subject)
이게 is the contracted form of 이것이.

지금 다시 생각해 보면, 학교 다닐 때가 좋았던 것 같아요.
Come to think of it, I think I was happy when I was going to school.

학교 = school
다니다 = to go, attend

부럽다

to be jealous, envious

ⓒ🅯🄯 *Eliza Mária Sándor*

부러워하다
to envy; to be jealous of

-아/어/여하다 is used at the end of some adjectives to change them into verbs to express one's feeling or describe how one treats others.

눈 = eye

부러운 눈으로 보다
to look at with envious eyes

부럽죠?
You envy me (him/her), right?

부러워요.
I envy you.

별로 안 부러워요.
I'm not particularly envious.

부러워하지 마세요.
Don't be envious.

부러워할 필요가 없어요.
There is no need to be jealous.

-(으)ㄹ 필요 없다 = to not need to + V

현우 씨를 왜 부러워해요?
Why are you envious of Hyunwoo?

왜 = why; for what reason; how come

윤아 씨가 부럽지 않아요?
Aren't you jealous of Yoona?
Don't you envy Yoona?

효진 씨가 그렇게 부러워요?
Do you envy Hyojin that much?

새 핸드폰을 샀더니 친구들이 부럽대요.
My friends say they are jealous of me because I bought a new cellphone.

새 = new
핸드폰 = mobile phone
사다 = to buy
-대요 = I heard that + S + V; They say + S + V

다른 건 안 부러운데 그거 하나는 부러워요.

I don't envy you, but that one thing, I am jealous of.

다른 = other; another
그거 = that
하나 = one (native Korean number)

다른 사람의 성공을 너무 부러워하지 마세요

Don't be too envious of another person's success.

성공 = success

저는 그림을 잘 그리는 사람이 너무 부러워요.

I really envy people that draw well.

그림 = drawing, painting, picture
그리다 = to draw, paint

그 일이 얼마나 편할까 생각하니 정말 부러워요.

As I think about how comfortable that work is, I am really jealous.

얼마나 = how + adjective/adverb
편하다 = to be comfortable; to be convenient
생각하다 = to think

그렇게 부러우면 윤아 씨도 그거 사면 되잖아요.

If you are that envious, Yoona, you can just buy it, too.

-(으)면 되다 = to be just supposed to + V; to just have to + V; can just + V

저도 모르게 부러운 눈으로 그 사람을 쳐다봤어요.

I look at that person with envious eyes without even noticing it.

모르게 = without knowing; without meaning to + V
쳐다보다 = to look (at); to stare

하고 싶은 일을 하고 있는 사람들이 제일 부러워요.

I am most envious of people that are doing what they want to do.

일을 하다 = to work
-고 있다 = to be + V-ing
제일 = the best; the most

부러워하지 마세요. 현정 씨도 곧 대학생이 될 거예요.

Don't envy them. You, Hyunjeong, will also be a university student soon.

곧 = soon
대학생 = university student
되다 = to become

친구가 얼마 전에 로또에 당첨 됐는데 정말 부러웠어요.

My friend won that lottery a little while ago, and I was really jealous.

얼마 전 = a while ago; the other day
로또 = lotto, lottery
로또(에) 당첨 되다 = to win a lottery

Week 10

만들다

to make

손으로 만들다
to hand-make something

책으로 만들다
to make (a story) into a book

음식을 만들다
to make food

이거 만들 줄 알아요?
Do you know how to make this?

다 만들면 말해 주세요.
Let me know once you are done making it.

이거 누가 만들었어요?
Who made this?

그거 손으로 만든 거예요.
It's handmade.
I made it with my hands.

저는 그런 거 못 만들어요.
I can't make such a thing.

이거 제가 직접 만든 거예요.
I made this myself.

이번에 새 명함을 만들었어요.
I made a new business card recently.

친구랑 떡볶이를 만들어 봤어요.
I tried making some tteokbokki with my friend.

손 = hand

책 = book

음식 = food

이거 = this thing; this
-(으)ㄹ 줄 알다 = to know how to + V

다 = all; every (thing)
다 -(으)면 = once + S + finish/done + V-ing
말하다 = to talk; to say; to speak; to tell
-아/어/여 주세요 = (polite) Please do + something + for me

누가 = who; someone (subject)

그거 = that

저 = (polite) I; me
그런 = (something) like that; such + noun
못 = can't

제 = (polite) my; I
직접 = directly; by oneself; with one's own hands

이번에 = this time; recently
새 = new
명함 = business card

친구 = friend
떡볶이 = tteokbokki; boiled rice cakes and fish cakes in a spicy sauce
-아/어/여 보다 = to try + V-ing

어떻게 이렇게 빨리 만들었어요?
How did you make it so quickly?

어떻게 = how
이렇게 = like this, in this manner; so +adjective
빠르다 = to be fast
빨리 is an adverb form of 빠르다.

이거 만드는 방법 좀 알려 주세요.
Tell me how to make this.

방법 = method, way
좀 = a little; please
알려 주다 = to let someone know; to teach something to someone
-(으)세요 = (polite) imperative

제가 만든 김치 볶음밥 맛이 어때요?
How does the kimchi fried rice that I made taste?

김치 볶음밥 = kimchi fried rice
맛 = taste
어때요? = how is + N?; used to suggest, propose, or offer something

그 사람의 이야기를 책으로 만들었어요.
They made his story into a book.

그 = the; that
사람 = person, people
이야기 = story; what one says

어제 찍은 사진으로 비디오를 만들었어요.
I made a video with the photos I took yesterday.

어제 = yesterday
(사진을) 찍다 = to take (photos)
사진 = photo
비디오 = video

제가 실수를 해서 괜히 일을 더 만들었어요.
I made a mistake and created more work.
I made a silly mistake and made the task more daunting.

실수 = mistake
실수를 하다 = to make a mistake
-아/어/여서 = because, since
괜히 = needlessly; in vain; uselessly
일 = work; task; thing, stuff; occasion
더 = more
일을 만들다 = to make trouble
일을 더 만들다 = to make the work/trouble bigger

음식을 먹을 줄은 아는데 만들 줄은 몰라요.
I know how to eat food, but don't know how to make it.

-(으)ㄹ 줄 모르다 = to not know how to + V

오늘 저녁에 손님이 오셔서 음식을 많이 만들어야 해요.
There will be some guests coming this evening, so I have to make a lot of food.

오늘 = today
저녁 = evening; dinner
손님 = guest; visitor
오시다 = (honorific) to come
많다 = to be a lot
많이 is an adverb form of 많다.
-아/어/여야 하다 = should; have to; must

제가 제일 좋아하는 감독이 이번에 새 영화를 만들었어요.

My favorite director recently made a new movie.

제일 = the best; the most
좋아하다 = to like
감독 = director
영화 = movie

이유
reason

개인적인 이유
personal reason

개인적이다 = to be personal; to be private
개인적인 is the adjective form of 개인적이다.

이유를 묻다
to ask the reason

묻다 = to ask

이유를 대다
to give a reason

이유가 뭔가요?
What is the reason?

뭐 = what; something
뭐 is the contracted form of 무엇.

지각한 이유가 뭐예요?
What is the reason you were late?
Why were you late?

지각하다 = to be late

아무 이유 없이 그냥 좋아요.
I just like (something/someone) for no reason.

아무 = (not) any
없다 = to not have, not exist; to be not there
그냥 = just, only, simply
좋다 = to be good, likable; to be desirable; to be nice; to like

---

이유가 뭔지 절대 말을 안 해요.
He won't say what the reason is at all.

절대 = never
말 = language; what one says; expression; word; term
안 = not
말을 하다 = to speak; to talk; to tell; to say

이유가 뭐냐고 물으면 어떻게 하죠?
What should I do if he asks what the reason is?

-냐고 is used when quoting or delivering what someone has asked.
-(으)면 = if + S + V; when/once + S + V
하다 = to do

정당한 이유도 없이 회사에서 잘렸어요.
I was fired from the company without a justifiable reason.

정당하다 = to be reasonable, to be fair; to be justifiable
정당한 is the adjective form of 정당하다.
-도 = too, also
회사 = company; office
잘리다 = (informal) to get fired; to get cut

그렇게 그 사람을 미워하는 이유가 뭐예요?

What is the reason you hate that person so much?

그렇게 = like that; such + adjective/adverb
그 사람 = that person; he, she
미워하다 = to hate, dislike

폭력은 어떤 이유로도 정당화 될 수 없어요.

Violence cannot be justified by any reason.

폭력 = violence
어떤 = what kind of; which
정당화 되다 = to be justified
-(으)ㄹ 수 없다 = to be unable to + V, can't

가장 어리다는 이유로 귀여움을 듬뿍 받았어요.

I received a lot of attention because of the fact I was the youngest.
People liked me a lot because I was the youngest.

가장 = the most
어리다 = to be young
귀여움(을) 받다 = to be favored or liked by someone

그 이유 때문인지 다른 이유 때문인지 모르겠어요.

I don't know if it is because of that reason or another.

때문이다 = it is because (of) ...
다른 = other; another
- 때문인지 - 때문인지 모르다 = to not know if it's because of + N₁ + or + N₂

그 사람이 그렇게 행동한 데에는 다 이유가 있어요.

There is a reason as to why he acted that way.

행동하다 = to act, behave
-(으/느)ㄴ 데(에) = in + V-ing, for + V-ing
있다 = to be there; to exist; to have

전화 할 때마다 전화기가 꺼져 있는 이유가 뭐예요?

What is the reason your phone is turned off every time I call?

전화(를) 하다 = to call, make a phone call
-(으)ㄹ 때마다 = whenever + S + V
전화기 = telephone
꺼져 있다 = to be turned off

제가 오늘 늦은 데에는 어쩔 수 없는 이유가 있어요.

I couldn't do anything about the reason I was late to work today.

늦다 = to be late
어쩔 수 없다 = can't help, can't but; there is nothing + S + can do about

그 사람이 그렇게 인기가 있는 건 다 이유가 있어요.

There is a reason why he is so popular.

인기가 있다 = to be popular

타당한 이유가 있으면 부모님이 허락해 주실 거예요.

If there is an appropriate reason, your parents will give you permission.

타당하다 = to be appropriate; to be reasonable
타당한 is the adjective form of 타당하다.
부모님 = parents
허락하다 = to allow, to give a permission
-아/어/여 주시다 = (honorific) someone does something for me/us

그 사람이 여기에 오지 않은 이유를 저는 알고 있어요.

I know the reason why he did not come here.

여기 = here, this place
오다 = to come
알다 = to know
-고 있다 = to be + V-ing

죄송하지만 개인적인 이유라서 자세히 말씀드릴 수가 없어요.

I'm sorry, but I cannot tell you specifically because it is a personal reason.

죄송하지만 = I'm sorry, but ...
-(이)라서 = because + S + be + N
자세하다 = to be specific, detailed
자세히 is an adverb form of 자세하다.
말씀드리다 = (polite) to talk; to say; to speak; to tell
-(으)ㄹ 수가 없다 = to be not able to + V, can't

입다

to wear (clothes)

ⓒ🅯🅭 *Eliza Mária Sándor*

갈아입다
to change (one's clothes)

옷을 입다
to wear clothes; to put on clothes

옷 = clothes, outfit

바지를 입다
to wear pants; to put on pants

바지 = pants

잠옷을 입다
to wear pajamas; to put on pajamas

잠옷 = pajamas

뒤집어 입다
to wear (clothes) inside out

뒤집다 = to turn something inside out; to flip

정장 입고 오세요.
Wear a suit/dress.

정장 = suit

그 옷 잘 어울려요.
You look good in that outfit.

잘 = well
어울리다 = to suit, match

이 옷 입어 봐도 돼요?
Can I try this on?

이 = this
-아/어/여도 되다 = to be okay to + V

뭐 입고 갈지 정했어요?
Have you decided what to wear?

정하다 = to decide

옷을 좀 더 따뜻하게 입으세요.
Wear warmer clothes.

따뜻하다 = to be warm
따뜻하게 is the adverb form of 따뜻하다.

거기는 어떤 옷 입고 가야 돼요?
What kind of clothes do I have to wear when I go there?

거기 = there
어떤 = what kind of

가다 = to go; to leave
-아/어/여야 되다 = to have to + V

티셔츠를 뒤집어 입은 것 같아요.
I think you are wearing your t-shirt inside out.

티셔츠 = t-shirt
- 것 같다 = It seems/looks like + S + V

저기 노란 옷 입은 사람 누구예요?
Who's that person in the yellow shirt?

저기 = there
노랗다 = to be yellow
노란 is the adjective form of 노랗다.
누구 = who

이 옷 입어 봤는데 좀 큰 것 같아요.
I've just tried this on, but I think it's a little too big for me.

크다 = to be big; to be tall; to be loud
큰 is the adjective form of 크다.

지금 그 옷 입기에는 너무 덥지 않아요?
Isn't it too hot to wear those clothes?

지금 = now
-기에 = (to be too + adjective) + to + V
너무 = too much, excessively; very
덥다 = to be hot

입을 옷이 별로 없어서 옷 사러 가려고요.

I don't have many clothes to wear, so I am going shopping for clothes.

별로 = not particularly, not very, not so much, not really
사다 = to buy
-(으)러 가다 = to go to + V

한 번 입었는데 벌써 이렇게 더러워졌어요.
I've worn this just once and it already got dirty like this.

한 번 = once, one time
벌써 = already
더럽다 = to be dirty
-아/어/여지다 = to become + adjective

지금 입고 있는 티셔츠는 어디에서 샀어요?
Where did you buy the t-shirt you are wearing now?

어디 = where; somewhere

옷이 더러워져서 그대로는 못 입을 것 같아요.

My clothes got dirty, so I don't think I can wear them.

그대로 = as it is, without changing anything

인터넷 쇼핑몰에서는 옷을 사기 전에 입어 볼 수가 없어요.
On Internet shopping malls, you can't try on clothes before you buy them.

인터넷 = the Internet
쇼핑몰 = shopping mall
-기 전에 = before + S + V

실패

failure

ⓒ①◎ 진석진

실패의 원인
cause of failure

원인 = cause

_____

실패하다
to fail

_____

사업에 실패하다
to fail in business

사업 = business

_____

실패로 돌아가다
to end in failure

_____

목표 달성에 실패하다
to fail in achieving one's goal

목표 = goal, aim, target
달성 = achievement, accomplishment

_____

이번에도 실패예요.
It's a failure again this time.

이번 = this; this time

_____

한 번도 실패한 적 없어요.
I have not failed once.

-(으)ㄴ 적 없다 = to have never p.p.

_____

실패를 두려워하지 마세요.
Do not be afraid of failure.

두려워하다 = to be afraid of, scared of

_____

다이어트에 또 실패했어요.
I failed my diet again.

다이어트 = diet; losing one's weight by putting in effort
또 = again

_____

처음에는 실패하는 게 당연해요.
It is natural to fail in the beginning.

처음 = first; for the first time
-것이 당연하다 = to be natural to + V; to be reasonable to + V

_____

성공할 줄 알았는데 실패했어요.
I thought I would succeed, but I failed.

성공하다 = to succeed
-(으)ㄹ 줄 알았는데 = I thought + S + was going to be + adjective but ...; I thought + S + would + V + but ...

실패의 원인이 뭐라고 생각해요?
What do you think the reason is for failing?

생각하다 = to think

오늘 처음으로 빵을 만들어 봤는데 실패했어요.
I tried making bread for the first time, but I failed.

처음으로 = for the first time
빵 = bread
만들다 = to make

실패할 걱정을 많이 하면 시작도 할 수가 없어요.
If you worry a lot about failing, then you cannot even start.

걱정을 하다 = to worry
시작하다 = to start, begin

이번 프로젝트는 성공할 줄 알았는데 또 실패로 끝났어요.
I thought I would succeed at this project, but it ended up a failure again.

프로젝트 = project

이번 학기에는 학점 4.3을 받는 게 목표였는데 실패했어요.
My goal was to get a 4.3 GPA this semester, but I failed.

학기 = semester
학점 = school credits; grade (in school)
받다 = to receive

올해 초에 세운 다섯 가지 목표 중 두 개는 벌써 실패했어요.
I already failed in (achieving) the two goals out of the five I set in the beginning of this year.

올해 = this year
초 = beginning of
세우다 = to set up; to make something stand
목표를 세우다 = to make a goal
다섯 = five (native Korean number)
가지 = kind (of)
중 = among; between; out of
둘 = two (native Korean number)
두 is the adjective form of 둘.
개 is a general counter for inanimate objects.

유명 배우들이 많이 나왔는데도 그 영화는 흥행에 실패했어요.
The movie failed at the box office even though a lot of famous actors starred in it.
That movie was a flop even though there were many famous actors in it.

유명 배우 = famous actor/actress
-들 is a suffix used to indicate plural.
나오다 = to come out
흥행 = big success of a movie

저희 회사에서 오랫동안 준비한 프로젝트가 실패로 돌아갔어요.

The project that our company prepared for a long time was a failure.

The project, which our company spent a long time preparing, ended up a failure.

저희 = (polite) we; us; our
오랫동안 = for a long time
준비하다 = to prepare; to get ready

오늘 아침에는 일찍 일어나서 운동을 하려고 했는데 늦잠을 자서 실패했어요.

I was going to wake up early and exercise this morning, but I overslept and (ultimately) failed.

아침 = morning; breakfast
일찍 = early; soon
일어나다 = to wake up; to get up
운동 = exercise; sports
운동을 하다 = to exercise, work out; to play a sport
-(으)려고 하다 = to plan to + V; to think of + V-ing; to mean to + V
늦잠을 자다 = to get up late, oversleep, sleep in

열다
to open

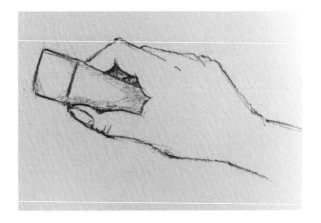

문을 열다
to open a door

문 = door

파일을 열다
to open a file

파일 = file; folder

마음을 열다
to open one's mind

마음 = heart; mind

뚜껑을 열다
to open a lid

뚜껑 = lid; cover; cap (of a lens/pen)

문 좀 열어 주세요.
Open the door for me, please.

이 열쇠로 열면 돼요.
You can open it with this key.

-(으)면 되다 = to be just supposed to + V; to just have to + V; can just + V

이거 열어 봐도 돼요?
Can I open this?

-아/어/여도 되다 = to be okay to + V

냉장고를 열어 보세요.
Open the refrigerator.

냉장고 = refrigerator

이 파일 어떻게 열어요?
How do I open this file?

전시회를 열 계획이에요.
I'm planning to open an exhibition.

전시회 = exhibition
계획 = plan
-(으)ㄹ 계획이다 = to plan to + V

뚜껑을 열어 놓지 마세요.
Don't leave the lid open.

-아/어/여 놓다 = to leave something in a certain state

아침 10시에 문을 열어요.
They open at 10 in the morning.

세 번째 서랍 열어 보세요.
Open the third drawer.

까페를 여는 것이 꿈이에요.
Opening a cafe is my dream.

지난 달에 새 가게를 열었어요.
We opened a new store last month.

가게를 열자마자 유명해졌어요.
The store became famous as soon as it opened up.

그 사람이 마침내 입을 열었어요.
That person finally spoke up.

저 도착했는데 문 좀 열어 주세요.
I've arrived. Open the door for me.

창문을 열자마자 벌이 들어왔어요.
As soon as I opened the window, a bee came in.

그 사람은 좀처럼 마음을 열지 않아요.
That person simply won't open his/her mind.

아침 10시 = 10 A.M.
문을 열다 = to open (a store/restaurant/etc); to open the door

세 번째 = third

까페 = cafe
꿈 = dream

지난 달 = last month
가게 = store, shop

-자마자 = as soon as + S + V
유명하다 = to be famous

마침내 = finally
입 = mouth
입을 열다 = to start talking; to speak up; to open one's mouth

도착하다 = to arrive

창문 = window
벌 = bee
들어오다 = to come in

좀처럼 = rarely, hardly; not easily
마음을 열다 = to open one's mind

성공

success

ⓒ①⑩ *Hyunwoo Sun*

대성공
a great success

성공 사례
an example of success

사례 = case, example

성공 요인
main factor of success

요인 = main factor

성공의 비결
secret to success

비결 = secret

성공하다
to succeed

성공적이다
to be successful

성공을 기원하다
to wish one success

기원하다 = to wish, pray

성공 비결이 뭐예요?
What is your secret to success?

성공적으로 잘 끝냈어요.
I finished it successfully.

끝내다 = to finish; to get + N + done

이번 공연은 성공적이었어요.
This time, the performance was successful.

공연 = performance, concert

이번 공연의 성공을 기원할게요.
I wish for the success of this concert.

-(으)ㄹ게요. = I promise I will + V.; I will + V.

그 사람은 분명히 성공할 거예요.
That person will definitely succeed.

분명히 = for sure, certainly, without doubt
-(으)ㄹ 것이다 = will; to be going to + V

이번 프로젝트는 대성공이었어요.

This project was a great success.

운이 좋아서 성공한 사람은 별로 없어요.

운 = luck
운이 좋다 = to be lucky

There are not many people who succeeded because they were lucky.

성공 사례들을 잘 보면 공통점이 있어요.

보다 = to see; to look; to watch; to meet up; to read
공통점 = things in common, common factors

If you carefully look at some examples of success, there are common factors.
If you look hard at examples of success, there are things in common.

성공하고 싶으면 그냥 열심히 하면 안 돼요.

-고 싶다 = to want to + V
열심히 = (to do something) hard; diligently
-(으)면 안 되다 = shouldn't; must not

If you want to succeed, you must not only work hard.

성공할지 실패할지는 해 보기 전에는 몰라요.

-(으)ㄹ지 -(으)ㄹ지 = whether to + V_1 + or to + V_2
전 = before, ago

Whether you will succeed or fail, you will not know before you try it.

이 계획이 성공하지 못 해도 다음 계획이 있어요.

-아/어/여도 = even though; no matter how much + S + V
다음 = next

Even if this plan is not successful, I have a plan B.

이번 프로젝트는 성공할 가능성이 충분히 있어요.

가능성 = possibility
충분하다 = to be enough, sufficient
충분히 is an adverb form of 충분하다.

This project has sufficient potential to succeed.

그 영화는 흥행에는 성공했는데 나쁜 평을 많이 받았어요.

나쁘다 = to be bad
나쁜 is the adjective form of 나쁘다.
평 = criticism; comment; review

That movie had a successful run at the box office, but it received a lot of criticism.

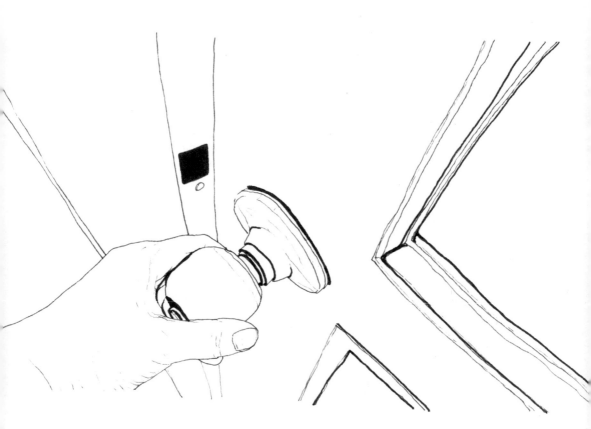

닫다

to close

ⓒⓕⓞ 마법사

문을 닫다
to close the door; to go out of business

뚜껑을 닫다
to close the lid

창문을 닫다
to close the window

문 닫고 들어오세요.
Please come in and close the door.

은행은 몇 시에 문을 닫아요?
What time does the bank close?

은행 = bank
몇 시 = what time

추워요. 창문 좀 닫아 주세요.
It's cold, please close the window.

춥다 = (place) to be cold; to feel cold

더운데 왜 창문을 닫아 뒀어요?
Why do you keep the window closed even though it's hot?
It's hot, so why is the window still closed?

왜 = why; for what reason; how come
-아/어/여 두다 = to leave something in a certain state

그 가게는 밤 11시에 문을 닫아요.
That store closes at 11 at night.

밤 = night
11시 = eleven o'clock

펜을 다 쓰면 뚜껑을 꼭 닫아 주세요.
When you finish using the pen, please make sure to put the cap back on.

펜 = pen
쓰다 = to use; to spend (+ money)
꼭 = for sure; at any cost; certainly; definitely; make sure to (do something); tight

제가 좋아하는 식당이 문을 닫았어요.
The restaurant that I like went out of business.

식당 = restaurant; cafeteria
식당 means "restaurant", but the word "레스토랑" refers to fancier or more upscale restaurants than "식당."

물병의 뚜껑을 꽉 안 닫아서 물이 샜어요.
Since I didn't close the cap on the water bottle tightly, the water leaked out.

물병 = water bottle
꽉 = fully; tight
물 = water
새다 = to leak

여기는 문을 닫았으니까 다른 곳으로 가
요.

This place is closed, let's go to a different place.

곳 = place
-아/어/여요 = imperative; Let's + V

냄비 뚜껑을 닫아 두면 물이 더 빨리 끓
어요.

If you keep the lid of the pot closed, the water boils
faster.

냄비 = pot
끓다 = to boil

나오기 전에 창문 다 닫았는지 확인해 주
세요.

Before going out, please check if you closed all the
windows.

-았/었/였는지 = probably because + S + V-ed;
whether + S+ V-ed
확인하다 = to check

아기가 자고 있으니까 문을 조심히 닫아
주세요.

Since the baby is sleeping, please carefully close the door.

아기 = baby
자다 = to sleep
조심하다 = to be careful
조심히 is the adverb form of 조심하다.

바람 들어오니까 들어올 때 문을 꽉 닫
아 주세요.

Since the wind is coming in, close the door all the way
when you come in.

바람 = wind
-(으)ㄹ 때 = when/while + S + V

문 닫지 마세요. 환기시키려고 열어 놓
은 거예요.

Don't close the door. I kept it open to circulate the air.

환기시키다 = to circulate the air
-(으)려고 = in order to + V
열다 = to open

그 가게는 인테리어 공사를 하려고 한 달
간 문을 닫는대요.

I heard that store is closing for a month to have the
interior renovated.
They say that store is closing for one month to have
interior construction.

인테리어 = interior
공사 = construction
공사를 하다 = to do construction work; to
construct
(amount of time) + -간 = for, during
-대요 = I heard that + S + V; They say + S + V

어제 문 닫는 걸 잊었나 봐요. 아침에 오니까 문이 열려 있었어요.

I must have forgotten to close the door yesterday. The door was open when I came in the morning.

가게에 손님이 오셨는데 문 닫을 시간이 다 되어서 돌려보냈어요.

Customers came to the store, but since it was time to close, I sent them back out.

잊다 = to forget
-았/었/였나 보다 = S + must have + p.p.; It seems like + S + V-ed
-아/어/여 있다 is used to express the continuing state of a completed action(past continuous).

시간 = time; hour
시간이 되다 = time is up
돌려보내다 = to send someone back

닫다

Week 11

Day 1   **Audio Track : 71**

사다 [sa-da]

to buy

Day 2   **Audio Track : 72**

약속 [yak-ssok]

plans; promise

Day 3   **Audio Track : 73**

팔다 [pal-da]

to sell

Day 4   **Audio Track : 74**

부족 [bu-jok]

shortage, lack, insufficiency

Day 5   **Audio Track : 75**

알다 [al-da]

to know

Day 6   **Audio Track : 76**

밥 [bap]

food; meal; cooked rice

Day 7   **Audio Track : 77**

모르다 [mo-reu-da]

to not know

사다
to buy

옷을 사다
to buy clothes

옷 = clothes, outfit

밥을 사다
to treat someone to a meal

밥 = food; meal; cooked rice

사다 주다
to buy something for someone and bring it to that person

주다 = to give

사다 놓다
to buy something and keep it for later use

놓다 = to place, put; to let go

싸게 샀어요.
I bought it for a low price.

싸다 = to be cheap
싸게 is the adverb form of 싸다.
싸게 사다 = to buy something for a low price

뭐 살 거예요?
What are you going to buy?

뭐 = what; something
뭐 is the contracted form of 무엇.
-(으)ㄹ 것이다 = will; to be going to + V

얼마에 샀어요?
How much did you pay for it?

얼마 = how much
(price)에 사다 = to buy at + (price)

어디에서 샀어요?
Where did you buy it?

어디 = where; somewhere

이거 사고 싶어요.
I want to buy this.

이거 = this thing; this
-고 싶다 = to want to + V

약 좀 사다 주세요.
Could you buy me some medicine and bring it to me?

약 = pill; medicine
좀 = a little; please
-(으)세요 = (polite) imperative

언제 밥 살 거예요?
When are you going to treat me to a meal?

언제 = when
밥을 사다 = to treat someone to a meal

여기서는 사지 마세요.
Don't buy it here.

여기서 = here, from here
-지 마세요. = (polite) Don't + V.

이거 사면 하나 더 드려요.
If you buy this, I'll give you another one for free.

-(으)면 = if + S + V; when/once + S + V
하나 = one (native Korean number)
더 = more
드리다 = (honorific) to give

이거 사고 나면 돈이 없어요.
If I buy this, I won't have any money left.

-고 나면 = once + S + finish + V-ing
돈 = money
없다 = to not have, not exist; to be not there

마음에 안 들어서 안 샀어요.
I didn't like it, so I didn't buy it.

마음 = heart; mind
마음에 들다 = to like
안 = not
-아/어/여서 = because, since

그 옷을 사고 나서 후회했어요.
I regretted buying those clothes.

그 = the; that
-고 나서 = after + S + V
후회하다 = to regret

인터넷으로 옷을 처음 사 봤어요.
This was my first time buying clothes on the Internet.

인터넷 = the Internet
처음 = first; for the first time
-아/어/여 보다 = to try V-ing

살까 말까 고민하다가 안 샀어요.
I was debating whether to buy it or not, and I ended up not buying it.

-(으)ㄹ까 말까 = whether to + V
고민하다 = to debate; to try to decide; to worry
-다가 = as a result of V-ing

할인 기간일 때 많이 사 놔야 해요.
You should buy a lot of things during the discount period. While the sale is going on, you should buy a lot of stuff (so you can use it later.)

할인 = sale, discount
기간 = period (of time), term
-(으)ㄹ 때 = while/when + S + V
많다 = to be a lot
많이 is an adverb form of 많다.
사 놓다 = to buy something (and keep it for later use)
-아/어/여야 하다 = should; have to; must

친구 선물로 뭐 살지 고민 중이에요.
I'm thinking about what to buy as a present for my friend.

친구 = friend
선물 = gift, present
뭐 -(으)ㄹ지 고민하다 = to try to decide what to + V
중이다 = to be V-ing; to be between/middle/in the middle of + V-ing

WEEK 11 DAY 2

약속
plans; promise

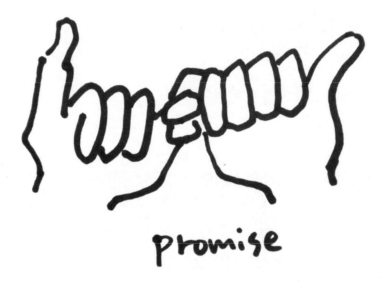

promise

ⓒⒾⓄ *CCKorea*

약속 시간
a time for meeting someone

시간 = time; hour

약속이 있다
to have something to attend; to have plans; to have an appointment

있다 = to be there; to exist; to have

약속을 지키다
to keep one's promise

지키다 = to keep; to guard

약속을 어기다
to break one's promise

어기다 = to break (one's promise)

약속을 취소하다
to cancel an appointment; to cancel plans

취소하다 = to cancel

약속할 수 있어요?
Can you promise?

약속하다 = to promise, make a promise
-(으)ㄹ 수 있다 = can, to be able to; there is a chance that + S + V

약속 지킬 수 있어요?
Can you keep your promise?

약속 꼭 지키실 거죠?
You are going to definitely keep your promise, right?

꼭 = for sure; at any cost; certainly; definitely; make sure to (do something); tight

약속 장소가 어디예요?
Where are you going to meet them?
Where are you supposed to go (to meet someone)?

장소 = place; venue

약속 시간에 또 늦었어요.
I'm late for an appointment again.

또 = again
늦다 = to be late

친구와 점심 약속이 있어요.
I have a lunch date with a friend.

점심 = lunch

제가 언제 그런 약속을 했어요?

When did I make such a promise?

지키지 못 할 약속은 하지 마세요.

Don't make a promise that you can't keep.

다시는 거짓말 안 한다고 약속할게요.

I promise you that I won't lie again.

약속이라도 한 듯이 모두 다 지각했어요.

As if everyone had planned it together, they were all late.

저는 오늘 약속이 있어서 먼저 가 볼게요.

I need to go somewhere today, so I'm going to go now.

친구하고 약속했기 때문에 안 가면 안 돼요.

I promised my friend, so I have to go.
I made a promise to my friend, so I can't skip out.

오늘 저녁에 친구와 약속이 있는 걸 깜빡 잊어버렸어요.

I completely forgot that I was supposed to meet my friend this evening.

이번 일요일에는 다른 약속이 있어서 못 만날 것 같아요.

I have something else to do this Sunday, so I don't think I can meet you.

오늘은 너무 피곤해서 약속을 취소하고 집에서 쉬었어요.

I was very tired today, so I cancelled my plans and got some rest at home.

제 = (polite) my; I
그런 = (something) like that; such + noun
약속을 하다 = to promise, make a promise

못 = can't

다시는 = (not) again
거짓말 = lie
거짓말 하다 = to lie

-라도 한 듯 = as if + S + V-ed
모두 = all; every; everyone
다 = all; every (thing)
지각하다 = to be late

저 = (polite) I; me
오늘 = today
먼저 = first; before + N
가다 = to go; to leave

때문에 = because (of), since
-(으)면 안 되다 = shouldn't; must not

저녁 = evening; dinner
깜빡 잊어버리다 = to completely forget about something (for a short period of time)

이번 = this; this time
일요일 = Sunday
다르다 = to be different
다른 is the adjective form of 다르다.
만나다 = to meet (up)
-(으)ㄹ 것 같다 = I think + S + will/be going to; it seems like + S + will/be going to

---

너무 = too much, excessively; very
피곤하다 = to be tired, exhausted; to be tiring
집 = house, home
쉬다 = to take a break; to get some rest

My Weekly Korean Vocabulary Book 1

팔다

to sell

꽃을 팔다
to sell flowers

꽃 = flower

_____

사고 팔다
to buy and sell

사다 = to buy

_____

싸게 팔다
to sell at a low price

_____

비싸게 팔다
to sell at a high price

비싸다 = to be expensive
비싸게 is the adverb form of 비싸다.

_____

이건 안 팔 거예요.
I am not going to sell this.

이건 = this (subject)
이건 is the contracted form of 이거는.

_____

저한테 그거 파세요.
Sell it to me.

그거 = that

_____

이거 어디에서 팔아요?
Where do they sell this?

_____

더 싸게 파는 곳 있어요?
Is there a place where they sell it at a cheaper price?

곳 = place   .

_____

그거 얼마에 팔 거예요?
How much are you going to sell it for?

_____

그거 팔지 말고 저 주세요.
Don't sell it and (instead) give it to me, please.

_____

그 가게에서 파는 꽃은 비싸요.
The flowers they sell at that shop are expensive.

가게 = store, shop

_____

이건 돈을 많이 줘도 안 팔 거예요.
Even if someone gives me a lot of money, I'm not going to sell it.

-아/어/여도 = even though; no matter how much + S + V

My Weekly Korean Vocabulary Book 1

헌 책 팔 수 있는 곳 알고 있어요?
Do you know a place where I can sell used books?

헌 = old, used, second-hand
책 = book
알다 = to know
-고 있다 = to be + V-ing

오늘은 비가 와서 많이 못 팔았어요.
It rained today, so I couldn't sell many things.

비 = rain
오다 = to come

예쁜 옷 싸게 파는 데 좀 알려 주세요.
Tell me some places where they sell pretty clothes at cheap prices.

예쁘다 = to be pretty
예쁜 is the adjective form of 예쁘다.
-는 데 = place where + S + V
알려 주다 = to let someone know; to teach something to someone

지금 살고 있는 집을 팔고 이사갈 거예요.
I'm going to sell the house I'm living in and move out.

지금 = now
살다 = to live
-고 있다 = to be + V-ing
이사가다 = to move out

카메라 싸게 파는 데 있으면 알려 주세요.
If you know a place where they sell cameras at cheap prices, let me know.

카메라 = camera

이 카메라를 팔고 새 카메라를 살 거예요.
I am going to sell this camera and buy a new one.

새 = new

제가 만든 목걸이를 인터넷으로 팔 거예요.
I'm going to sell the necklace that I made on the Internet.

만들다 = to make
목걸이 = necklace

원래 만 원인데 오늘만 오천 원에 팔고 있어요.
It's normally 10,000 won, but for today only, I'm selling it for 5,000 won.

원래 = originally; normally
만 = ten thousand
-만 = only; just
오천 = five thousand

부족

shortage, lack, insufficiency

Eliza Mária Sándor

수면 부족
lack of sleep; sleep deprivation

수면 = sleep

경험 부족
lack of experience

경험 = experience

운동 부족
lack of exercise

운동 = exercise; sports

부족하다
to lack; to be short of; to be insufficient

음식 안 부족해요?
Would you like more food?

음식 = food

여기 의자가 하나 부족해요.
We are short of a chair here.

여기 = here, this place
의자 = chair

부족한 게 있으면 말씀하세요.
If you are lacking anything, tell us.
Let us know if there's a shortage of anything.

-(으)면 = if/when + S + V, once + S + V
말씀하다 = (honorific) to talk; to say; to speak; to tell

요즘 잠이 너무 부족해서 피곤해요.
I am tired because I am really lacking sleep these days.

요즘 = these days, lately
잠 = sleep

부족한 게 많지만, 열심히 준비했어요.
I am lacking a lot, but I diligently prepared.

열심히 = (to do something) hard; diligently
준비하다 = to prepare; to get ready

이번 프로젝트는 준비가 너무 부족해요.
This project lacks a lot of preparation.

프로젝트 = project
준비 = preparation

하고 싶은 일은 많은데 시간이 부족해요.

I have a lot of things I want to do, but there is not a sufficient amount of time.

하다 = to do
일 = work; task; thing, stuff; occasion

꼭 사고 싶은 책이 있는데 돈이 부족해
요.

There is a book I really want to buy, but I am short of money.

자리가 부족하니까 옆으로 좀 비켜 주세
요.

There's not enough space, so please move to the side a little.

자리 = space, spot, seat, position; occasion
-(으)니까 = since, because
옆 = next
-아/어/여 주세요 = (polite) Please do + something + for me.

경은 씨는 노래는 잘하는데 자신감이 부
족해요.

Kyeong-eun sings well, but lacks self-confidence.

노래 = song
잘하다 = to be good at something
자신감 = confidence

보고서를 완성해야 하는데 자료가 너무
부족해요.

I have to finish the report, but the data is really insufficient.

보고서 = report
완성하다 = to finish, complete, get something done
자료 = data; material

돈이 부족하다고 해서 행복하지 않은 건
아니에요.

Just because one has an insufficient amount of money, it doesn't mean one is unhappy.

-다고 해서 = since someone says/said ...
행복하다 = to be happy

머리가 아파서 병원에 갔더니 수면 부족
이 원인이래요.

I went to the hospital because my head hurt, and they said the cause was lack of sleep.

머리 = head; hair
아프다 = to be sick, hurt
병원 = hospital
-더니 = S + V-ed + and as a result
원인 = cause
-래요 = I heard ...; They said ...

그 사람은 실력은 있는데 아직 어려서 경
험이 부족해요.

That person has the skills, but lacks experience since he is still young.

그 사람 = that person; he, she
실력 = skill, ability
아직 = (not) yet
어리다 = to be young

오늘은 꼭 고백을 하려고 했는데 용기가
부족해서 못 했어요.

I really wanted to confess (my feelings) today, but I
couldn't because I lacked the courage.

제 컴퓨터에 저장하려고 했는데 용량이
부족해서 못 했어요.

I was going to save it on my computer, but I couldn't
because there was insufficient memory.

고백 = confession
고백을 하다 = to confess
-(으)려고 하다 = to plan to + V; to think of +
V-ing; to mean to + V
용기 = courage

컴퓨터 = computer
저장하다 = to save
용량 = capacity; volume

알다
to know

아는 사람
a person one knows; an acquaintance

잘 알다
to know well

제가 알기로는
from what I understand; as far as I know

대충 알아요.
I know roughly.

대충 = approximately, roughly; not thoroughly

이제 알겠어요.
Now I understand it.

이제 = now

그걸 어떻게 알아요?
How do you know that?

그걸 = that, that thing (object)
그걸 is the contracted form of 그것을.
어떻게 = how

아는 척 하지 마세요.
Don't pretend you know.; Don't act as if you know.

- 척 하다 = to pretend

윤아 씨가 알 수도 있어요.
Yoona might know.

-(으)ㄹ 수도 있다 = may/might + V; can/could + V

알면서 왜 모른 척 했어요?
Why did you pretend not to know when you do (actually) know?

-(으)면서 = while + S + V-ing
왜 = why; for what reason; how come
모르다 = to not know

답을 알면 빨리 알려 주세요.
If you know the answer, tell me quickly.

빠르다 = to be fast
빨리 is an adverb form of 빠르다.

제 친구 통해서 알게 됐어요.
I learned (about it) through my friend.

통해서 = through, via
-게 되다 = will + V (unintetionally); to get to + V; to end up + V-ing

전화번호 좀 알 수 있을까요?
Can I know the phone number?
Can I get the phone number?

전화번호 = phone number

왜 알면서도 말을 안 했어요?
Why didn't you tell me when you knew?

-(으)면서도 = even though; (even) while; even when
말 = language; what one says; expression; word; term
말을 하다 = to speak; to talk; to tell; to say

비밀번호는 효진 씨만 알아요.
Only Hyojin knows the password.

비밀번호 = password

혹시 석진 씨 전화번호 알아요?
Do you, by any chance, know Seokjin's phone number?

혹시 = by any chance

그 일에 대해서라면 제가 잘 알아요.
When it comes to that (subject), I know a lot about it.
I know about that (subject) well.

-에 대해서라면 = about + N; when it comes to + N

그 사람이 어디 있는지 알 것 같아요.
I think I know where he is.

모두가 알고 있었는데 저만 몰랐어요.
Everyone (already) knew, but I was the only one who did not know.

제가 알기로는 그 사람은 지금 출장 중이에요.
From what I know, that person is now on a business trip.

출장 = business trip
중 = in, in the middle of

어제 영화관에서 우연히 아는 사람을 만났어요.
I bumped into a person I know in the movie theater yesterday.

어제 = yesterday
영화관 = movie theater, cinema
우연히 = by chance
우연히 만나다 = to bump into someone

밥

food; meal; cooked rice

아침 밥
breakfast

아침 = morning; breakfast

_____

저녁 밥
supper

_____

볶음밥
fried rice

볶다 = to stir-fry

_____

비빔밥
bibimbap; mixed rice

비비다 = to mix; to rub

_____

밥을 먹다
to eat; to have a meal

먹다 = to eat; to drink

_____

밥을 굶다
to skip a meal

굶다 = to skip a meal; to starve

_____

밥을 하다
to cook; to make steamed rice

밥을 하다 = to cook a meal; to make food; to cook steamed rice

_____

아침 밥 먹었어요?
Did you have breakfast?

_____

밥 먹으러 갈래요?
Do you want to go eat?

-(으)러 가다 = to go to + V

_____

밥 먹고 산책 가요.
Let's go for a walk after eating.

산책 = walk
산책 가다 = to go for a walk

_____

밥 한 그릇 더 주세요.
Give me one more bowl of rice, please.

한 is the adjective form of 하나.
그릇 = dish, bowl

밥 먹다가 말고 어디 가요?
Where are you going in the middle of a meal?

-다 말고 = while + S + is in the middle of + V-ing

저녁에 비빔밥을 먹었어요.
I had some bibimbap for dinner.

비빔밥 = bibimbap; steamed rice mixed with vegetable (and some meat depending on the type) with red pepper paste

밥을 못 먹어서 배가 고파요.
I haven't eaten, so I am hungry.

배 = stomach, belly
배가 고프다 = to be hungry

다음 주에 같이 밥 먹을까요?
Shall we meet up and eat together next week?

다음 = next
주 = week
같이 = together; with + N
-(으)ㄹ까요? = Shall we + S + V?; Do you want me to + V?; Should we + V?; Let's + V.

밥 너무 많이 먹는 거 아니에요?
Aren't you eating too much?

배 고프죠? 제가 지금 밥 할게요.
You must be hungry! I will make some food for you now.

너무 바빠서 밥 먹는 것도 잊어버렸어요.
I was very busy, so I even forgot to eat.

바쁘다 = to be busy
잊어버리다 = to forget

다이어트 하느라 하루 종일 밥을 굶었어요.
I am on a diet, so I skipped meals all day long.

다이어트 하다 = to be on a diet
-느라 = for + V-ing, while + V-ing
하루 = one day
하루 종일 = all day long

밥 먹을 때에는 텔레비전을 끄면 안 될까요?
Can we turn off the television while we are eating?

텔레비전 = television
끄다 = to turn off
-(으)면 안 될까요? = Can/Can't we ...?

모르다
to not know

ⓒⓕⓞ 송미진

모르는 사람
a person who one doesn't know; a stranger

모르는 번호
a phone number that one doesn't recognize

번호 = number
번호 is often used when referring one's phone number.

모르는 이야기
something that one has not heard of before; a story that one has not heard before

이야기 = story; what one says

저는 잘 모르겠어요.
I don't know.; I'm not sure.

저만 몰랐던 거예요?
So, only I didn't know?

-던 것이다 is a sentence ending that expresses a fact which was previously not revealed.

누구인지 모르겠어요.
I don't know who that is.

누구 = who
-(느)ㄴ지 is a verb ending that comes before words such as "to know," "to ask," "to not know," "to find out," etc, to show what the speaker is referring to.

모르는 척 하지 마세요.
Don't pretend that you don't know.

저는 모르는 이야기예요.
I don't know what you are talking about.

저도 이 동네는 잘 몰라요.
I don't know this neighborhood that well, either.

이 = this
동네 = neighborhood

어디에 있는지 모르겠어요.
I don't know where it is.

아직은 모르는 척 해 주세요.
For now, please pretend that you don't know about it yet.

아직은 = (not) yet

아직 모르는 게 좋을 거예요.
It'll be better for you not to know about it yet.

좋다 = to be good, likable; to be desirable; to be nice; to like

모르는 번호로 전화가 왔어요.
I received a phone call from a number that I don't know.

전화 = phone call; telephone
전화가 오다 = to get a phone call

그 사람은 모르는 것이 없어요.
There is nothing he doesn't know.

것 = thing

몰라도 괜찮아요. 물어보면 돼요.
It's okay if you don't know. You can just ask.

-아/어/여도 괜찮다 = to be okay to + V
물어보다 = to ask
-(으)면 되다 = to be just supposed to + V; to just have to + V; can just + V

어디에 가야 살 수 있는지 몰라요.
I don't know where I need to go to buy this.

-아/어/여야 -(으)ㄹ 수 있다 = to have to + V₁ + to be able to + V₂

아무리 생각해 봐도 답을 모르겠어요.
No matter how much I think about it, I still don't know the answer.

아무리 = no matter + adjective/adverb
생각하다 = to think
답 = answer; correct answer; reply

모르는 게 있으면 저한테 물어보세요.
If there is something that you don't know, please ask me.

이야기하느라 시간 가는 줄 몰랐어요.
We were busy talking, so we didn't notice the passage of time.

이야기하다 = to talk, speak, say, tell; to have a conversation; to tell a story
-는 줄 모르다 = to not know/notice + S + V

모르는 사람을 함부로 따라가면 안 돼요.

You shouldn't carelessly follow a stranger.

함부로 = carelessly
따라가다 = to follow

Week 12

주다
to give

벌을 주다
to give a punishment; to punish

벌 = punishment

상을 주다
to give a prize

상 = prize; award

선물로 주다
to give as a present

선물 = gift, present

먹을 것을 주다
to give something to eat; to feed

먹을 것 = food, something to eat
먹을 것 literally means "thing to eat," but it is a set expression that refers to food in general.

더 주세요.
Please give me more.

더 = more
-(으)세요 = (polite) imperative

저도 주세요.
Please give me (some), too.

저 = (polite) I; me
-도 = too, also

힌트 좀 주세요.
Give me some hints.

힌트 = hint; heads-up
좀 = a little; please

그 책 좀 주세요.
Please give me that book.

그 = the; that

시간을 좀 더 주세요.
Please give me a little more time.

시간 = time; hour

어제 꽃에 물 줬어요?
Did you give water to the flowers yesterday?
Did you water the flowers yesterday?

어제 = yesterday
꽃 = flower
물 = water

저도 같은 걸로 주세요.
Give me the same one.
I will have the same one.

같다 = to be the same
같은 is the adjective form of 같다.

지금 사면 하나 더 준대요.

I heard if you buy it now, they will give you one more.

지금 = now
사다 = to buy
-(으)면 = if/when + S + V, once + S + V
하나 = one (native Korean number)
-대요 = I heard that + S + V; They say + S + V

엄마, 책 사게 돈 좀 주세요.

Mom, please give me some money so that I can buy books.

엄마 = mom
-게 = so that + S + can + V
돈 = money

그거 친구가 선물로 줬어요.

My friend gave me that as a present.

그거 = that
친구 = friend

그거 어제 저한테 안 주셨어요.

You didn't give me that yesterday.

안 = not

이거 제가 작년에 준 장갑 아니에요?

Aren't these the gloves I gave you last year?

이거 = this thing; this
제 = (polite) my; I
작년 = last year
장갑 = glove
아니다 = to be not

목이 너무 말라서 그러는데 물 좀 주세요.

I'm thirsty, so please give me some water.

목 = throat; neck
너무 = too much, excessively; very
목이 마르다 = to be thirsty

작년에 제가 준 책 아직도 다 안 읽었어요?

You still have not finished the book I gave you last year?

아직도 = still, (not) yet
읽다 = to read

친구가 콘서트 티켓을 줘서 어제 보고 왔어요.

My friend gave me concert tickets, so I went and watched it yesterday.

콘서트 = concert
티켓 = ticket
-아/어/여서 = because, since
보다 = to see; to look; to watch; to meet up; to read
-고 오다 = to go do something and then come back

친구한테 선물로 주려고 샀는데 너무 마음에 들어서 그냥 제가 쓸 거예요.

I bought it to give it to my friend as a present, but I like it so much that I will just use it myself.

-(으)려고 = in order to + V
마음에 들다 = to like
그냥 = just, only, simply
쓰다 = to use; to spend (+ money)
-(으)ㄹ 것이다 = will; to be going to + V

사랑

love

ⓒⓕⓞ 신문희

첫사랑
first love; puppy love

첫 = first (of something)

_____

짝사랑
one-sided love; a crush

_____

사랑하는 사람
a person one loves

사람 = person, people

_____

사랑하다
to love

_____

사랑 받다
to be loved

받다 = to receive

_____

사랑에 빠지다
to fall in love

빠지다 = to fall out (of something); to fall in
(to something); to drown; to be dropped; to
be hooked

_____

사랑을 고백하다
to confess one's love

고백하다 = to confess

_____

사랑에 눈이 멀다
to be blinded by love

눈 = eye
눈이 멀다 = to be blind; to go blind

_____

사랑해요.
I love you.

_____

사랑이 뭐예요?
What is love?

뭐 = what; something
뭐 is the contracted form of 무엇.

_____

첫사랑 이야기해 주세요.
Tell me about your first love.

이야기 = story; what one says
이야기를 하다 = to talk, speak, say, tell; to have
a conversation; to tell a story
-아/어/여 주세요. = (polite) Please do + something + for me.

My Weekly Korean Vocabulary Book 1

사랑하는 사람이 생겼어요.
I have someone that I love now.

생기다 = to come into being; to be created; to appear; to be formed

---

윤아 씨가 제 첫사랑이에요.
Yoona is my first love.

사랑한다는 말을 많이 하세요?
Do you say the words "I love you" a lot?

말 = language; what one says; expression; word; term
말을 하다 = to speak; to talk; to tell; to say
많다 = to be a lot
많이 is an adverb form of 많다.

여자는 사랑에 빠지면 더 예뻐진대요.
They say women become more attractive when they fall in love.

여자 = girl, woman
예쁘다 = to be pretty
-아/어/어지다 = to become + adjective

경화 씨가 저 사랑한다고 고백했어요.
Kyeong-hwa confessed that she loves me.

-다고 = just because; saying that + S + V

노래 가사에는 사랑 이야기가 많아요.
There are many love stories in song lyrics.

노래 = song
가사 = lyrics

사랑하는 제 동생이 이번 여름에 결혼을 해요.
My beloved brother is getting married this summer.

동생 = younger sister/brother
이번 = this; this time
여름 = summer
결혼을 하다 = to get married

이 세상에서 저는 저희 부모님을 가장 사랑해요.
(Out of all the people) In this world, I love my parents the most.

이 = this
세상 = world
저희 = (polite) we; us; our
부모님 = parents
가장 = the most

사랑하는 사람 때문에 종교를 바꾸는 사람도 있어요.
There are people that convert religions because of the people they love.

때문에 = because (of), since
종교 = religion
바꾸다 = to change
있다 = to be there; to exist; to have

받다
to receive

상을 받다
to win an award; to receive a prize

벌을 받다
to be punished; to receive punishment

주고 받다
to exchange; to give and take

주다 = to give

전화를 받다
to answer the phone

전화 = phone call; telephone

선물을 받다
to receive a gift

월급을 받다
to get a salary

월급 = salary, monthly paycheck

이메일을 받다
to receive an e-mail

이메일 = e-mail

제 문자 받았어요?
Did you get my text message?

문자 = text message; letter, character

나쁜 일을 하면 벌 받아요.
If you do bad things, you get punished.

나쁘다 = to be bad
나쁜 is the adjective form of 나쁘다.
일 = work; task; thing, stuff; occasion
나쁜 일을 하다 = to do something bad
벌 받다 = to be punished

제가 보낸 이메일 받았어요?
Did you receive the e-mail I sent you?

보내다 = to send; to spend (time)

오늘 학교에서 상 받았어요.
I got a prize at school today.

오늘 = today
학교 = school

졸업 선물로 노트북을 받았어요.
I got a laptop computer for my graduation present.

졸업 = graduation
노트북 = laptop computer

항상 받기만 해서 너무 미안해요.
I feel bad that I always just receive (things/help) from you.

항상 = always, all the time
-기만 하다 = just + V; to only + V

아까 전화 했는데 왜 안 받았어요?
Why didn't you answer the phone when I called you earlier?

아까 = before, earlier
전화하다 = to call, make a phone call
왜 = why; for what reason; how come

이번 생일에 선물을 많이 받았어요.
I got a lot of presents for my birthday.

생일 = birthday

이번 생일에 무슨 선물 받고 싶어요?
What gift do you want for your birthday this year?

-고 싶다 = to want to + V

저는 하루에 수십 통의 이메일을 받아요.

I get dozens of e-mails a day.

하루 = one day
수십 = dozens of
- 통 is a counter for phone calls/letters/e-mails/bottles.

오늘 월급 받았어요. 제가 맛있는 거 사 줄게요.
I got paid today. I'll treat you to something delicious.

맛있다 = to be delicious
맛있는 is the adjective form of 맛있다.
맛있는 거 = something delicious, delicious food
사 주다 = to buy something for someone

수업 시간에 친구와 문자를 주고받다가 선생님께 혼났어요.
I was scolded by my teacher for texting my friend during class.

수업 = class
주고받다 = to give and receive
-다가 = as a result of + V-ing
선생님 = teacher
혼나다 = to get scolded

외국에 있는 친구에게 1주일 전에 편지를 보냈는데 오늘 받았대요.
I sent a letter to my friend who is staying overseas a week ago, and she said she got it today.

외국 = foreign country
1주일 = one week
전 = (polite) I (subject)
편지 = letter

연락

contact

연락처
contact information; phone number

연락을 하다
to contact

하다 = to do

연락을 받다
to hear from someone

연락이 끊기다
to lose touch (with someone)

끊기다 = to be cut

연락을 주고받다
to keep in touch; to stay in contact

곧 연락할게요.
I will contact you soon.

곧 = soon

연락하고 지내요.
Let's keep in touch.

지내다 = to live; to spend (time)

연락처 좀 알 수 있을까요?
Can I have your contact information?

알다 = to know
-(으)ㄹ 수 있다 = can, to be able to; there is a
chance that + S + V
-(으)ㄹ까요? = Shall we + S + V?; Do you want
me to + V?; Should we + V?; Let's + V.

늦게 간다고 연락했어요?
Did you call them (and tell them) you were going to be
late?

늦다 = to be late
늦게 is the adverb form of 늦다.
가다 = to go; to leave

가끔 연락 주고받고 있어요.
We keep in touch and talk once in a while.

가끔 = sometimes

집에 도착하면 연락 주세요.
Contact me when you get home.

집 = house, home
도착하다 = to arrive

이 전화 번호로 연락 주세요.
Contact me at this phone number.

전화 번호 = phone number

요즘 그 사람하고 연락 돼요?
Have you been in touch with him lately?

요즘 = these days, lately
그 사람 = that person; he, she
되다 = to be done; to be possible; (something) works

오시기 전에 미리 연락 주세요.
Let me know before you come for a visit.

오다 = to come
-기 전에 = before + S + V
미리 = in advance; beforehand

지금 조금 바쁘니까 나중에 연락할게요.
I'm a little busy now, so I will contact you later.

조금 = a little
바쁘다 = to be busy
나중에 = later

더 일찍 연락 드리지 못 해서 죄송합니다.
I'm sorry that I didn't contact you earlier.

일찍 = early; soon
드리다 = (honorific) to give
못 = can't
죄송합니다. = (polite) I'm sorry.

영국에 유학 간 친구에게서 연락이 왔어요.
I heard from my friend who is studying abroad in England.

영국 = The United Kingdom; England; Great Britain
유학 가다 = to go abroad to study
연락이 오다 = to hear from someone

그 사람하고는 연락이 끊긴 지 오래 됐어요.
It's been a while since I lost touch with him.

연락이 끊기다 = to lose touch with someone
-(으)ㄴ 지 오래 되다 = to have been a long time since

더 궁금하신 점이 있으면 바로 연락 주세요.
Please contact us right away when you have any further questions.

궁금하다 = to be curious
점 = point; aspect
바로 = right away; straight; exactly; close(ly); right; none other than

---

그 사람 전화 번호를 집에 두고 와서 지금은 연락할 방법이 없어요.
I've left his phone number at home, so there is no way I can contact him now.

집에 두고 오다 = to leave (something) at home and come (to a place); to leave (something) behind at home
방법 = method, way
없다 = to not have, not exist; to be not there

원하다
to want

원하는 물건
something you want to have; a desired item

물건 = thing, stuff; item; belonging

원하는 대로
as one wants; as one wishes

간절히 원하다
to desire eagerly; to long for; to yearn for

간절하다 = to be eager; to be desperate
간절히 is the adverb form of 간절하다.

원하는 게 뭐예요?
What is it that you want?

원하는 만큼 가져가세요.
Take as much as you want.

-(느)ㄴ 만큼 = as much as one + V
가져가다 = to take

원하지 않으면 저 주세요.
If you don't want it, give it to me.

원하시면 이것도 가져가세요.
If you want, take this as well.

이것 = this; this thing

원하는 게 있으면 빨리 말해요.
If you have something you want, hurry up and tell me.

빠르다 = to be fast
빨리 is an adverb form of 빠르다.
말하다 = to talk; to say; to speak; to tell
-아/어/여요 = imperative; Let's + V

제가 원하는 건 이런 게 아니에요.
This is not the kind of thing I want.
This is not what I want.

이런 = N + like this

저도 제가 뭘 원하는지 모르겠어요.
I also don't know what I want.

뭘 = what (object)
뭘 is the contracted form of 무엇을.
모르다 = to not know

아이가 원하는 대로 하게 놔 두세요.
Let the kid do what he/she wants.

아이 = child, kid; baby
-게 놔 두다 = to let + person + V

원하시면 제가 차로 데려다 드릴게요.
If you want, I can take you there by car.
If you want, I can drive you there.

차 = car
데려다 드리다 = (honorific) to take someone to + place

원하는 대로 안 된다고 화내지 마세요.
Don't get angry just because things don't go as you want.

화내다 = to be angry at someone; to yell at someone out of anger
-지 마세요 = (polite) Don't + V

그 사람은 항상 원하는 게 너무 많아요.
He always desires too much.

사람들은 누구나 행복해지기를 원해요.
Everyone wants to be happy.

-들 is a suffix used to indicate plural.
누구나 = anyone, anybody
행복하다 = to be happy
-아/어/여지다 = to become + adjective

돈이 많으면 원하는 것을 다 할 수 있나요?
Can you do anything you want if you have a lot of money?

다 = all; every (thing)
(으)ㄹ 수있다 = can, to be able to; there is a good chance that + S + V

아이들이 어떤 선물을 원하는지 물어봤어요?
Did you ask what kind of presents the children want?

어떤 = what kind of; which

원하는 종류의 기사만 모아서 보여주는 앱이 있대요.
There is a (mobile) app for gathering and displaying only the types of articles you want.

종류 = kind, sort, type (of)
기사 = (news) article
-만 = only; just
모으다 = to gather; to save up
-아/어/여서 = by + V-ing; to + V + and (then)
보여주다 = to show, display
앱 = app, application

여기는 제가 원하는 책을 싼 값에 살 수 있어서 좋아요.
This place is good because I can buy the books I want at a cheap price.

여기 = here, this place
싸다 = to be cheap
싼 is the adjective form of 싸다.
값 = price
좋다 = to be good, likable; to be desirable; to be nice; to like

이 레스토랑에서는 원하는 만큼 음식을 먹을 수 있어요.

In this restaurant, you can eat as much food as you want.

레스토랑 = restaurant

A Korean word for a "restaurant" is "식당," but when you use "레스토랑" instead of "식당," it usually refers to a fancy or upscale restaurant that sells western-style cuisine, including Italian or French. Even if a restuarant is very fancy and expensive, if it's a Korean, Japanese, or Chinese restaurant, normally the word "레스토랑" is not used.

먹다 = to eat; to drink

문자

text message

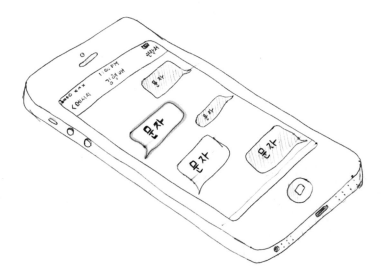

문자 메시지
text message

메시지 = message

문자를 받다
to get a text message

문자를 씹다
to ignore one's text message

씹다 is a slang expression that means "to ignore one's text message, or what one says."

문자를 보내다
to send a text message; to text

문자를 주고받다
to send text messages to each other

문자 주세요.
Send me a text message.

문자로 보내 주세요.
Tell me with a text message.

나중에 문자 보낼게요.
I'll text you later.

제 문자 왜 자꾸 씹어요?
Why do you keep ignoring my text messages?

자꾸 = repeatedly, again and again

장난 문자 보내지 마세요.
Don't send me phony text messages.

장난 = prank
장난 문자 = phony text message

연락처를 문자로 보낼게요.
I will send you my contact information via text message.

연락처 = contact; phone number

어제 제가 보낸 문자 보셨어요?
Did you see the text message I sent you yesterday?

보시다 = (honorific) to see; to look; to watch

해외에서도 문자 보낼 수 있어요?
Can you send text messages from overseas?

해외 = overseas

문자는 받았는데 아직 못 읽었어요.
I got the text message, but I haven't read it yet.

아직 = (not) yet

전화 통화가 안 돼서 문자 보냈어요.
I couldn't get through when I called you, so I sent a text message.

통화 = phone call, telephone conversation
안 되다 = S + doesn't work; can't + V

핸드폰 액정이 깨져서 문자를 못 읽어요.

The display screen on my cellphone is cracked, so I can't read text messages.

핸드폰 = mobile phone
액정 = display screen (usually for mobile phones)
깨지다 = to be cracked, broken

지금은 전화 못 하니까 문자로 보낼게요.

I can't call you right now, so I will send a text message.

-(으)니까 = since, because

그 사람은 문자 메시지를 참 재미있게 보내요.
His text messages are funny.

참 = very, quite
재미있다 = to be fun; to be funny; to be interesting
재미있게 is the adverb form of 재미있다.

핸드폰 문자 메시지를 너무 많이 써서 손이 아파요.
I've been texting too much, so my hands are sore.

문자를 쓰다 = to send text messages; to use text messaging service
손 = hand
아프다 = to be sick, hurt

저는 문자 쓰는 거 별로 안 좋아해요. 전화하는 게 편해요.
I don't really like texting. It's more convenient to call.

별로 = not particularly, not very, not so much, not really
좋아하다 = to like
편하다 = to be comfortable; to be convenient

빌리다

to borrow; to rent

Eliza Mária Sándor

돈을 빌리다
to borrow money

책을 빌리다
to borrow a book

책 = book

힘을 빌리다
to get (someone's) help

힘 = strength, power, energy

돈 좀 빌릴 수 있어요?
Can I borrow some money?

펜 하나만 빌려도 될까요?
Can I borrow a pen?

펜 = pen
-아/어/여도 될까요? = Can I/we + V?

만원만 빌릴 수 있을까요?
Do you think I could borrow 10,000 won?

만원 = 10,000 won

어제 빌린 돈 언제 갚을 거예요?
When are you going to pay me back the money that you borrowed yesterday?

언제 = when
갚다 = to pay back

도서관에 가서 책 좀 빌려 올게요.
I will go borrow some books from the library.

도서관 = library
-아/어/여 오다 = to go + V + and come back
-(으)ㄹ게요. = I promise I will + V.; I will + V.

친구한테 빌린 책을 잃어버렸어요.
I lost the book that I borrowed from a friend.

잃어버리다 = to lose + N

잠깐만 핸드폰 좀 빌릴 수 있을까요?
Can I borrow your cellphone for a minute?

잠깐 = short time; for a moment

그 사람은 돈을 빌리고 잘 안 갚아요.
He usually doesn't pay back the money he owes.

안 = not

이번 주말에 차 좀 빌릴 수 있을까요?
Can I borrow your car this weekend?

주말 = weekend

지난 일요일에는 DVD를 빌려 봤어요.
Last Sunday, I rented and watched some DVDs.

지난 = last
일요일 = Sunday

저번에 빌려 간 책은 언제 돌려주실 거예요?
When are you going to return the book that you borrowed last time?

저번에 = the other day; last time
돌려주다 = to return something to someone, give something back

지난번에 저한테서 만 원 빌린 거 잊었어요?
Did you forget that you borrowed 10,000 won from me last time?

지난번 = last time

밖이 너무 추워서 친구의 자켓을 빌려 입었어요.
It was too cold outside, so I borrowed my friend's jacket.

밖 = outside
춥다 = (place) to be cold; to feel cold
자켓 = jacket
입다 = to wear (clothes)

친구가 돈을 빌리고 한 달이 넘도록 갚지 않아요.
My friend borrowed some money and she hasn't paid me back for over a month.

한 달 = one month
넘다 = to be over + time/amount
-도록 = till, until, to the point where

오랜만에 만화책방에 가서 만화책을 빌려 봤어요.
I went to a comic book rental shop after a long time, and read some comic books.

오랜만에 = after a long time
만화책방 = comic book rental shop
만화책 = comic book

도서관에서 책을 빌렸는데 반납하는 걸 깜빡했어요.
I borrowed some books from the library, but I forgot to return (them).

반납하다 = to return something that one rented
깜빡하다 = to completely forget (for a short period of time)

친구가 노트북을 빌려 갔다가 돌려줬는데 고장이 났어요.
My friend borrowed my laptop computer and gave it back, but it is not working.

-았/었/였다가 = V-ed + and then
고장이 나다 = to break; to be broken